A Twentieth-Century Congress

by
ESTES KEFAUVER

and
Dr. JACK LEVIN

Foreword by
ROBERT M. LA FOLLETTE, JR.

DUELL, SLOAN AND PEARCE · NEW YORK

A TWENTIETH-CENTURY CONGRESS

A NOTE ABOUT THE AUTHORS

ESTES KEFAUVER

Member of Congress, Third District, Tennessee; Member, Committee on Judiciary; former Chairman, Sub-committee on Small Business.

DR. JACK LEVIN

Governmental economic consultant; Author of *Power Ethics* (1931), *Valuation and Regulation of Public Utilities* (with Dr. John H. Gray, 1933), and other works.

PREFACE

I CAME TO CONGRESS IN 1939 REPRESENTING THE THIRD TEN-
nessee District, and have served continuously since then.
Like many an average freshman congressman, I had my ideals
and plans for worthwhile legislation. I felt that the United
States soon would enter upon the world stage in a leading
role. I was anxious that Congress be equipped for the part
it would have to play.

As the years passed, the results were disappointing. I found
that outmoded legislative machinery made it difficult to get
much done. I soon realized that the Congress, intended by
the Founding Fathers to be the predominant branch of the
government, was ill equipped to chart the legislative program of the nation and was surrendering too many treasured
powers to the Executive. I also discovered that the numerous
other services expected of a congressman left me little time to
study or analyze legislation.

I do not believe the average citizen fully appreciates what
this means to him personally. I doubt if most people realize
the enormity of the burdens of congressmen or that they understand what clumsy tools we have with which to do our
work.

I hope this volume may be of some help to those who want
to see the federal legislature strong and able to cope intelligently with the increasing complexity of this advanced era.

I pay tribute to the able men responsible for the recent
excellent achievement in modernizing Congress. These in-

clude the chairman of the Joint Committee on the Organization of Congress, former Senator Robert M. La Follette, Jr., of Wisconsin, and his equally competent vice-chairman, Congressman A.S. Mike Monroney, of Oklahoma, and the other capable committeemen and members of Congress who led the fight for passage of the Legislative Reorganization Act of 1946. I especially pay tribute to George B. Galloway, who was staff director of the Joint Committee. Dr. Galloway and his associates in the Committee on Congress of the American Political Science Association have made an outstanding contribution to the efforts to improve the national legislature.

Charter Heslep, Washington manager of the Mutual Broadcasting System and former managing editor of the Washington *News,* deserves warmest praise and thanks. His wealth of information on the functioning of the government and his insight into practical politics have been drawn upon heavily.

I have asked Dr. Jack Levin, well-known author and capable attorney, to collaborate with me as a joint author of this volume. Since 1929, Dr. Levin has participated actively in federal legislative work in both branches of Congress, and for over a decade he has had responsible executive work in various branches of the national government.

I am also grateful for the helpful criticisms and suggestions of Dr. Charles A. Beard, Bernard M. Baruch, David Cushman Coyle, Dr. Ernest S. Griffith, David E. Lilienthal, Clifford J. Durr, Nathan Straus, former Governor Ellis G. Arnall, John B. Blandford, Jr., Edward J. Meeman, Dr. Frank Prescott, Dr. C. A. Dykstra, Senators J. William Fulbright, Joseph H. Ball, Harley M. Kilgore, and John Sparkman, and Congressmen Henry M. Jackson, Everett M. Dirksen, Christian A. Herter, Emanuel Celler, and Mike Mansfield, as well as former Congressmen George E. Outland and Charles M. La Follette. The suggestions and encouragement of George Fort Milton of the Buffalo *Evening News,* and Mrs. Katherine Stone, vice-president of the National League of Women Voters, are gratefully acknowledged.

While recognizing the excellent progress that has been made in the Legislative Reorganization Act of 1946, I am realistic. In the first place, the hands of a fine committee were tied by the resolution creating it. The members were expressly forbidden even to consider certain basic matters that go to the heart of any thorough repairing of ancient congressional machinery. Equally important, due to the wide divergencies of viewpoint existing among the members of the Joint Committee, only a part of the worthwhile suggestions that were made found a way into their report to Congress. Finally, even the recommendations of this diluted report were whittled down drastically by the political compromises that were essential if any reorganization bill was to pass at all. Consequently, the real job still remains.

There is a great deal of talk in responsible quarters of scrapping the heart of the present limited Reorganization Act. The people of the United States must realize at once the importance of not only holding onto what has been gained, but of going on to complete the job of modernizing what is still antiquated and inadequate congressional machinery. That is why this book was written.

ESTES KEFAUVER

Contents

FOREWORD

I AM HONORED BY THE INVITATION OF THE AUTHORS OF THIS
volume to write a foreword. The maintenance and modernization of representative government in the United States is
a matter of vital national concern. During my twenty-one
years of service in the Senate, vast economic and social developments have added heavy responsibilities to American
government at every level. And now the complex postwar
problems of maximum employment, world peace, and many
others that press for solution require modern and efficient
organization of government.

Students and many participants in politics alike, agree that
the whole machinery of our government requires reorganization if democracy is to meet the challenge of these demanding times. Reconstruction of the federal administrative structure dislocated by the war, the development of effective fed-
eral-state-local relationships in many fields, and the rapidly
expanding growth of relations between the United States
and the new international organizations are three areas of
obvious importance in the machinery of government. But
fundamental to all these under our constitutional system are
the role and relations of Congress.

Representative Kefauver and Dr. Levin make a very timely
and helpful contribution in this book to public understanding of the organization and operation of Congress. Informed
by personal experience and close observation and inspired by
a conscientious concern for good government, they give the
reader an authentic view of the machinery and methods of

our national legislature. They show that Congress, prior to the passage of the Congressional Reorganization Act of 1946, has not been well organized or adequately equipped to perform its lawmaking, appropriating, and supervisory functions under modern conditions. It has lacked adequate information and inspection facilities. Its internal structure has been antiquated. Its liaison with the Executive is irregular and spasmodic. Its surveillance of administrative performance has been sporadic and superficial. Much of its time has been consumed by petty local and private matters.

After describing what's wrong with Congress in graphic terms, the authors analyze current proposals for legislative reform and outline their own program for a "Twentieth-Century Congress." Without endorsing all of the authors' conclusions or all the reforms they advocate, it seems to me that their proposals for further modernization merit the careful consideration of members of the Congress and every citizen interested in the efficiency and effectiveness of American democracy.

Upon a stronger and more effective Congress may well depend the preservation of democracy in the United States. This book is dedicated to that end. I commend it, therefore, to the thoughtful consideration of the American people and hope that it will be widely read.

—Robert M. La Follette, Jr.

A TWENTIETH-CENTURY CONGRESS

CHAPTER 1

Is Congress Necessary?

Is CONGRESS NECESSARY?

Eighteen years of succeeding crises, first on a domestic and then on an international scale, have left many Americans uncertain as to the future role Congress is to have in the democratic system. For twelve of those years, beginning in 1933, there was an exceptionally strong, tough-minded, and glamorous Executive in the White House.

The crash of the stock markets late in 1929 raised the curtain on the greatest economic disaster this nation ever experienced. The failure of Congress, in whose hands the Constitution largely places the destiny of this nation, to provide inspired leadership or create effective measures to cope with the deepening depression, set the stage for an amazing decade in American history.

Paralyzing fear, aggravated by the breakdown of already inefficient and outmoded legislative machinery, rendered Congress so impotent that it was ready to sign away its constitutional birthright for any mess of pottage that would fill the shrinking stomachs of voters who clamored for bread in a land of plenty. Had Franklin Roosevelt really aspired to be the dictator that many later proclaimed he intended to be, that mess of pottage might have been the alphabetical soup concocted by the new Executive's talented brain trust. The people were in a mood to accept as a palatable substitute even for democracy any formula that would save their jobs, their homes and farms, and their lives.

This is no idle metaphor. Recall how often President Roosevelt, making skillful use of a new means of mass appeal, the radio, "went over the heads of Congress" to ask the people to support his proposals for recovery and reform. And how a sometimes reluctant Senate and House, unequipped to offer anything better, were forced to yield to the public's response to those "fireside chats." In so doing, the legislators surrendered what seemed vast grants of power to the executive branch of the government. We already are far enough removed from this period to see that actually Congress lost more prestige and self-respect than legislative sovereignty. Those multiple proposals rubber-stamped by a dazed Congress did not alter the fundamentals of the American government. Proof of this fact lies in the high percentage of those hastily enacted laws that passed the test of constitutionality before the Supreme Court. Unlike another strong, but in that case malevolent, leader in a nascent democracy beset by grave problems, our Executive did not demand goose-stepping, heils, and the absolutism of the *fuehrer* principle. That is fortunate. The people might have been tempted to try such nostrums.

Political rivalry always has made Congress an easy target for abuse by a partisan press when the party in power was of the opposite political faith from this or that group of editors. However, about a quarter-century ago, this criticism began to take on a more general character and to come from many sources. For two decades the national legislature has been subjected to an endless stream of ridicule, scorn, and even contempt. A generation has reached maturity with a dangerously cynical attitude toward the legislative process. Is it any wonder, then, that some of its members give serious thought to the possibility that Congress might *not* survive the next twenty years, especially if those years should bring national and worldwide emergencies such as have occurred since 1929?

Can Congress meet this challenge? Yes, it can, if boldly and intelligently it will do three things: *Examine its present faults; analyze the additional duties and responsibilities that a twentieth-century democracy imposes upon it; and take the necessary steps to permit the efficient discharge of both its old and new functions.*

What are these old and new functions? These must be understood clearly by all the people if the difficult task of modernizing the legislative branch of government is to have intelligent public support. The 1946 Reorganization Act, which will be examined in detail, was only a beginning. Congress today has vastly greater responsibilities than were envisioned by the framers of the Constitution. And the Founding Fathers devoted more time and language to defining the legislative functions than to all the other subjects covered in that original national charter.

Congress is the very heart of the American representative system of government. By whatever name it may be called, the legislature is the keystone of any form of democracy. Failure of the legislative branch to keep pace with the needs of the people it was constituted to serve, has brought death to many democratic governments.

When in 1933 some eighty million Germans said, in effect, that representative government was not necessary and acquiesced in the imposition of nazism, they unloosed a demon that quickly reduced a once-great nation to virtual slavery and sought to impose serfdom on the rest of the world.

Eleven years earlier, in 1922, the people of Italy had embraced the dictatorship of Mussolini's fascism and its corporate state because of the inability of their parliamentary system to function effectively. The *Cortes* of the Spanish Republic was unable to perfect legislative procedure to meet the needs of that nation: Iberian democracy perished before the onslaughts of the Falange and Franco after a bloody struggle.

Inspired by the idealism of America as symbolized by Woodrow Wilson, there were brave experiments in representative government in Central Europe following World War I. Peoples of existing and re-created nations sought to throw off the tyrannies of centuries and become their own masters, but only the competent Czechs were able to build a democracy that endured. Even France was in ferment when World War II broke out; powerful rightist and leftist groups were plotting to overthrow a parliamentary system rotting away because of the plague of multiple parties and archaic procedures.

Today, this United States is the greatest republican form of democracy left among the major powers. It is the bulwark for that philosophy which dignifies the individual citizen and proclaims the right of free enterprise. Its citizens are on the threshold of an era that may be even more revolutionary in its effect on their lives than the industrial revolution—the age of atomic energy. The face of the earth again may be changed—literally. The new dangers are breathtaking in their possible consequences.

The political mechanism of this country must be capable of grappling successfully with the many new and strange problems on the horizon of civilization. At the same time, those fundamental liberties which are the foundation of American democracy must be preserved. The bulk of this burden will rest with the legislative branch. Therefore, to get a proper perspective on the kind of Congress needed, we must define realistically and in terms not usually found in textbooks, the present scope of Congress. There are three broad divisions of congressional responsibility.

The first, and still the most important, is to determine after careful deliberation the metes and bounds of national policies and to pass the best possible laws to carry out those policies. This is the original and traditional function that is set out in detail in the ten sections of Article One of the Constitution.

For more than one hundred years, this basic duty required of conscientious members a thorough knowledge of the needs and aspirations of the people. In addition, they had to possess the ability to provide necessary legislation to aid the growth and prosperity of a rapidly expanding nation. Great national crises arose and were met successfully, although it took four years of bloody war to decide the issue of a permanent and indivisible union of what are now the forty-eight states.

Following the temporary emergence of the United States into world leadership in World War I, Congress, or rather the Senate, rejected the principle of global cooperation as symbolized by the League of Nations. America lapsed into the traditional isolationism that up to then had served this nation so well in its march to greatness. The next quarter-century proved how grave was this error. National policies such as higher tariffs, voted by Congress, helped to set in motion a worldwide depression. Through bitter experience, Congress learned that in more and more areas where heretofore members had to consider only how pending bills applied to this nation, it now had to study the effects of proposed policies on the entire world.

World War II dramatized the awful necessity for global thinking. Problems as local as commuter-train timetables had to be considered with a view to keeping tracks clear for supplies destined for battlefields around the world. The four-year political phenomenon of almost every major policy before the national legislature's having an international character did not end with V-E and V-J Days. At this time, issues such as merger of the armed services, atom-bomb control, world agricultural problems, foreign loans, and others, require of members of Congress knowledge and research undreamed of in the first century of the national legislature's existence. Even if no other functions had been added, it is obvious that Congress would need to throw off the trivia that have accumulated over the years.

Its members must have more time for deliberation and more facilities for information so as to reach decisions that not only stand the test of being the best from a national viewpoint but also take into account the prevailing international situation.

Once decisions are reached, the Congress, under the Constitution, is required to see that they are carried out in the spirit intended and that money voted to put policies in effect is spent properly. When the executive branch of the government was relatively small—and that would mean up to the past score of years—it was fairly easy to do this. Today, more and more discretion must be left to the executive departments. Where the law ends, and executive discretion begins, seems likely to be a moot point for a long time to come.

As national government functions expanded prodigiously, the amount of tax money necessary to carry on these new duties also climbed rapidly, as did the number of employees in the executive departments. This development has made it imperative, in the interest of good government, that the national legislature equip itself with modern methods of executive review and audit. It should also set up an efficient system of supervising executive rules and regulations. Only by doing so can it perform adequately and completely its main function of being responsible for the formulation and implementation of national policies.

The second great responsibility of members of Congress is to represent their respective states and districts. Here again, the work has grown in volume and importance as federal and state governments have become ever more interdependent. States' rights still are embedded in the Constitution and are a powerful weapon to use in warding off undue encroachments of a too-powerful central government. But it must be admitted that the area of operation of exclusively state functions of government has been narrowed drastically.

Take highways as an example. Although the Constitution provided that Congress might establish "post roads," this function for decades was almost wholly a local one. Today, the principle of matching state and federal monies for highway construction and maintenance has been in operation for many years. This same policy of providing funds ties Congress into many other fields that once were exclusively the province of state governments. The current legislative program for a billion-dollar national system of airports, and similar movements in a dozen other fields, impose upon members of Congress the added responsibility of seeing that their respective states or districts share equitably in these plans.

Federally financed public works once were limited mostly to river and harbor improvements and erection of post offices. In the lean and hungry nineteen-thirties, public works came to embrace almost every conceivable kind of project. Members of Congress must use influence to see that their constituents get a fair share of benefits from those programs. They must assemble influential delegations "from back home" and marshal imposing charts and statistics to impress some executive department with the claim of their particular constituency for—to use a current example—the location of a new veterans hospital.

Much of this increased federal operation in what once was deemed state domain can be traced to the progressively broadened interpretation of a single phrase in the Constitution, ". . . to regulate commerce . . . among the several States." Without going into a detailed account of how it came about, it suffices to say that the condition requires much more time and thought by individual members of Congress today than in earlier periods of congressional history.

The third great responsibility of members of Congress is relatively new. It is the one that has brought the greatest increase in the man-hours of labor required in congressional offices. It has not been adequately defined in any textbook. We refer to the role of the individual senator and congressman as the *personal* representative in Washington of individuals back in his state and district.

Many condemn this time-consuming, often seemingly trivial work as errand-boy stuff. It is true that some members become so engulfed in doing chores for their constituents that they hardly have time to perform their other more important duties. The condition is dangerous and must be faced boldly.

It would, however, be both impractical and unjust to demand that Congress as a body disregard the thousand-and-one personal requests for various services which the people, as individuals, impose upon its members. We say impractical, because to do so would invite defeat at the polls. We say unjust because, with the growth of a vast, impersonal government that daily touches so many points in the everyday life of the citizen, and with special groups of every kind organized in Washington to press their special interests, the individual voter has a right to have his own personal representative at the seat of government. No other official—public or private—is better qualified to perform that function than his elected senator or congressman.

Nevertheless, there are available many devices and business practices that can be put into effect to enable the members to handle this added work efficiently. Some of the suggestions we will make here, considered singly, might seem unimportant, but in total effect they are aimed at conserving the time and energy of Congress for its more important tasks without neglecting this vital service to the constituents. We shall study this problem from several angles, but let us first examine briefly the present structure and personnel of Congress and discuss previous attempts to meet changing conditions that have faced the institution from time to time.

What is Congress?

It is one of the three great branches of government set up by the Constitution; it is supported by taxes on the American public, and has been doing business since 1789, most of that time in the historic buildings assembled on a twenty-acre knoll in the District of Columbia, called Capitol Hill.

It now has 96 senators, two from each state, and 435 men and women in the "lower chamber," or House of Representatives. This averages about one member for each 300,000 citizens living in the 435 congressional districts in the 48 states on a population basis. A few districts embrace entire states; representatives chosen from them are called "members-at-large." There are some additional non-voting members of the House representing the territories and island possessions.

Of the 139,000,000 persons in the U.S.A. (Census Bureau 1946 estimates), the foregoing accounts legislatively for 138,000,000. The other million are the residents of the great city that is the seat of the national government, Washington,

D.C. They cannot even vote but are a special group of political orphans illogically deemed unable to exercise self-government and thrust, like unwanted stepchildren, in the lap of Congress.

Voters mark a ballot for a representative every two years and for a senator every six years. Most of the time the choice is limited to two persons, candidates selected respectively by the Democratic and Republican parties in each state, and usually nominated in party elections called primaries. Other parties appear on the ballot from time to time, elect some members or even put a candidate in the presidential race, but it is the Democrats and the Republicans who, election after election, present full slates of candidates and are generally referred to as the "major parties."

However, the exercise of the privilege of voting apparently doesn't make very much impression on a considerable portion of the public. In one large sampling of citizens, only 38 out of every 100 could name their own congressmen. (Can the reader?) Also, in too many states, too many people do not bother to vote, while in some others, because of suffrage restrictions, less than 10 per cent of the population does the electing.

Every year many thousands of citizens, especially young men and women, sit briefly on the uncomfortable benches in the visitors' galleries of the Senate and House; become bewildered and confused when they see only a handful of members making motions they do not understand; then leave to go home and ask their friends and neighbors: "What do those people do for the $12,500 a year we pay them?"

Despite the apathy of too large a segment of the population and some cruel handicaps deriving from a rigid two-party system, the voters send good men and women to Washington. That statement will be hooted by many readers. Far more thoughtless and uninformed criticism is hurled at the ability, character, and personality of the membership of Congress than at the obscure but more vulnerable targets of its archaic procedures, haphazard organization, diffused responsibility, and the habit of running in too many directions at once.

Congress has its share of crackpots, cheap publicity-seekers, shirkers, and chiselers. So has almost any organization of like size. However, impartial studies support our contention as to individual worth. Since any testimony of ours could be discounted as prejudiced, we rest our case with the findings of one of America's most respected historians, Dr. Charles A. Beard. In *The American Mercury*, Dr. Beard says:

"In their efforts to appear wise, critics of Congress often refer to the great of old . . . to orators like Webster, Calhoun and Clay—and assert that, in comparison, members of Congress today are of small caliber. It is true that no member now can, or chooses to, deliver orations in the grand manner. But is that proof of a decline in intelligence and character? In my opinion, it is nothing of the sort. . . . The truth is that oratory of the grand style, whatever its merits, if any, is no longer appropriate to or useful in the discussion of the complicated questions of our day, which call for highly specialized knowledge and less rhetoric.

"As a more than casual student of the *Congressional Record*, I venture this opinion: It is possible to pick out of the *Record* for the past ten years addresses (not orations) which for breadth of knowledge, technical skill, analytical acumen, close reasoning and dignified presentation, compare favorably with similar utterances made in the preceding century by the so-called great orators. Sweeping as this statement appears to be, I make the assertion and invite those who have recently been preaching the contrary to assume the burden of proving their contentions."

Dr. Beard further points out in this study that "the great scandals which have rocked the country during the past fifty years have all occurred in the executive department."

It is also a common practice to condemn the Congress as unrepresentative of the people and as being a "group of political lawyers" or merely a "bunch of lazy professional politicians." The latter charge is refuted by the conscientious and hardworking job that most members of Congress try to do.

A superficial glance at the vocations listed by the 531 legislators in the *Congressional Directory* might seem to confirm the first generalization. In the 79th Congress, more than 60 per cent of the Senate (62 out of 96) and over half of the House (241 out of 435) were lawyers. The next most numerous classifications, but far behind the bar, were businessmen (House, 47; Senate, 10); and editors, publishers, and journalists (House, 24; Senate, 10). However, the affinity of law and politics is a natural one since it is the duty of legislatures, be they city councils, state bodies, or Congress, to draft and pass laws. Since government is called upon to make decisions in the field of economics and business, many businessmen are elected. And since the press of the nation, now seconded by radio, largely interprets government to the people, the presence of a substantial group of men from journalistic professions is not surprising.

One group is conspicuous by its virtual absence. The rise in membership and power of organized labor has not resulted yet in any rush to the polls by labor to send its own men and women to Congress. This doubtless is due to a traditional policy not to engage in direct political action, a policy that is being challenged by the Congress of Industrial Organizations, arch-rival of the older American Federation of Labor. Farmers, listed as such, also are not as numerous as the power of the farm block would lead one to expect.

The listing by avocation is quite misleading, however, as

an indication of the representative character of the men and women on Capitol Hill. Many members who formerly were attorneys in rural areas and put "lawyer" after their name are as zealous in advancing the interest of the farm groups as any "dirt farmer" could hope to be. And most members have had pretty much the same experiences as the average American citizen. They have gone to the same schools and churches and joined the same lodges, civic organizations, and clubs. They see the same movies as the rest of the country, listen to the same variety of broadcasts, talk the same language, and place great store in tradition. In short, they *are* the rest of the country. That is why there is about the same proportion of outstanding, average, and lesser people in Congress as there is in any individual community.

And that is why we will spend no time condemning individuals or seeking rascals or scapegoats in our analysis of Congress. There are on the whole as good people in Congress as back home. What is important is that whoever is elected to the Senate and House have the greatest opportunity to become representative of all the people in his constituency, as well as of the nation as a whole. Voters will be able to see if congressmen do a job and to check on their promises when they come up for reelection, if congressional machinery is made thoroughly simple and modern. We will therefore attempt to suggest in this volume what needs to be done to complete the job so well begun by Congress when it took the first fine step forward with the Legislative Reorganization Act of 1946.

Having outlined briefly the "what" and "who" of the national legislature, we go back now to our opening question as to the necessity of Congress. Our answer is a loud and confident YES: Congress *is* necessary. If we had any mental reservations on that point, we never would have attempted the task of writing a book one of whose authors must in addition discharge his responsibilities as the Representative from the Third Congressional District of Tennessee.

CHAPTER 2

The Job Is Not Done

THE NEED FOR CONGRESS IS FAR MORE VITAL NOW THAN IT was when able gentlemen in knee breeches, lace, and three-cornered hats burned midnight candles in Philadelphia and wrote the Constitution. If the reader had lived then, he would hardly have been aware of the existence of the national government in everyday life. Today it regulates even the time: the clocks of the nation are set by the federally operated Naval Observatory in Washington. This relatively obscure fact is only a symbol of the vast expansion in governmental service that the people have demanded their Congress approve as modern science, industry, and education changed ways of living.

The Supreme Court still has only nine members. Congress increased slowly to its present membership of 531 as new states were admitted and population growth called for adding seats in the House. Almost all of the expansion in government has taken place in the executive department, headed by the President and his Cabinet. What is more important, the rate of this expansion of bureaus and departments has been increasing since the turn of this century, reaching amazing proportions in the past two decades. Yet most Americans do not perceive that every new function added to the executive branch increases the responsibility of Congress and adds many man-hours to the work that must be done on Capitol Hill. Likewise, each addition brings new burdens to the members of Congress individually.

There is no reversal of this trend in the offing. Government apparently is going to get bigger, not smaller; more complex, not simpler, regardless of what party happens to be in power. During 1946 the Senate and House had to wrestle with such problems as atomic energy, the merger of the armed forces, universal military training, world finance and rehabilitation, and strongly backed proposals for greater federal participation in housing, health, education, labor, and business. Most of these issues, and other equally important ones, will face succeeding Congresses.

All this means good laws are harder than ever to make because the subjects they cover are so much more difficult. In most major legislation, much discretion must be left to the executive departments in carrying out the policies laid down in the laws. This results in what has been decried as "personal government": thousands of rules and regulations, having the force of a law passed by Congress, but issued by some administrator or government bureau. This condition, a necessary technique for efficient modern government, imposes an additional and fundamental responsibility on Congress to be vigilant to protect the people's rights against the natural and human faults of bureaucracy.

The actual drafting of laws has become highly specialized and requires staffs of experts. Compare a five-hundred-page revenue bill of today with the simple federal excise tax laws of the early days. (And one of those brief statutes, a whisky tax, caused a small rebellion.) Clerks using quill pens hardly had to fear writer's cramp in drawing up the handful of appropriation bills for the First Congress, which in two years voted only $4,269,000. But adding machines and the latest business equipment were needed to put together the $262,-000,000,000 worth of appropriations measures enacted by wartime Congresses.

The people should demand that Congress make sure they get the best possible value received for these increasing billions of tax money invested every year in their government. During the war years, despite the valiant work of the Truman (later Mead-Kilgore) committee, Congress was, and still remains, pitifully unequipped to discharge this important duty. Too many of the headline-making probes become mere attempts to put a lock on a barn door after some rather expensive horses have been stolen.

Finally (and this concerns the third function of Congress previously mentioned), the citizen seldom knows more than a few of the persons in the government who have been given some power or duty that personally affects him or his business. So, each year, members get more thousands of letters from constituents asking information, assistance, and referral to the proper federal agency, registering protests, making suggestions, and so on. "Write your senator and congressman" has become a national habit rivaling in volume the exchange of Christmas cards, with this exception: the congressional mail comes three hundred sixty-five days of the year.

These increasing pressures on Congress are not something apart from the rest of the life of the nation. Rather are they the result of the fast pace of this twentieth century. The terrible and succeeding crises of the war just ended spurred on the impatient demand to get things "done yesterday." Americans became accustomed to a concentration of power and authority in almost all walks of life that was a necessary aspect of a nation totally mobilized for war. But even before the war, a decided trend toward "czars" and "bosses" was observable.

There are examples in trade organizations, business, labor, and even in sports. While each case differed, there seemed to be a surge to shelve regularly elected governing bodies that had worked well, in favor of powerful executives who "knew how to get things done."

This struggle for what might be called the survival of the deliberative function in society marked the greatest battle at the San Francisco Conference which blueprinted the United Nations. It was an epic and partially successful fight to preserve fundamental sovereign rights.

Don't sell this business of deliberation short. Most people have a more definite idea of the meaning of "life, liberty and the pursuit of happiness" today than they had before the Axis clutched at democratic throats in the dark moments of 1942. It is the great system of representative government, with the Congress as its policy-creating organ, that has enabled the American citizen to enjoy the widest possible individual freedom of thought and action as well as the collective security of a strong nation. The kind of progress that is going to endure lies in action taken and laws made after there has been a "meeting of the minds" of legislators chosen by the people.

Has the deliberative capacity of members of Congress deteriorated? We do not think so. Occasionally, when a senator or congressman somehow finds the time to work up a well-documented speech for a committee or the floor, the effort is worthy of the best traditions of statesmanship. The pity is that many members who have real contributions to make to the vital meeting of minds are so bogged down with office work and multiple meetings that they only make a showing for the record, or launch into debate without sufficient background or research. Consequently they often appear to critics of Congress to be men of little minds. "Thimble-brained" is a popular adjective assigned to them.

The greater evils lie in the outmoded and confused methods that hamstring Congress in executing both its traditional and its newer duties, and not in a degradation of the caliber of the men and women the people elect to the national legislature. Fortunately, remedies are at hand. We are no Jeremiah calling out in a wilderness. For the past decade, thoughtful lawmakers have been filing an increasing number of bills dealing with some aspects of the problem. This pressure resulted, early in 1945, in the creation of the Joint Committee on the Organization of Congress, headed by the late Senator Francis Maloney and, after his death, by Senator Robert M. La Follette, Jr., with Representative A.S. Mike Monroney as vice-chairman. Unwisely, we think, the scope of the inquiry was limited. Nevertheless, this committee produced one of the most important reports ever placed before the national legislature. The hearings before the group reveal that senators and congressmen presented more than two hundred sixty ideas for improving the present functioning of the legislative institution. The hearings, report, and the Legislative Reorganization Act (Public Law 601—79th Congress) deserve serious attention not only from students of government and the thirty-two hundred men and women employed to help run Congress, but from voters and citizens throughout the country.

The Joint Committee on the Organization of Congress was limited by the act creating it from making many basic recommendations; furthermore, it was unable to agree among its own members on reorganization matters within its jurisdiction; and finally, the limited recommendations it eventually did make were whittled away by the Senate and House through political bargaining and jockeying. There are tough foes to face in any reform movement. Despite the large number of individual members, especially those more recently elected to Congress, who sense the danger to American government in continuing with the remaining outmoded congressional customs, it will take active support from the voters to achieve a real streamlining on Capitol Hill. Perhaps some comparisons that demonstrate the vastly changed conditions now facing the national legislature will help to dramatize the issue. Without belittling the splendid achievement of the 79th Congress on reorganiaztion, there still remain many antiquated procedures that have not been altered materially since the Senate and House first opened for business.

George Washington needed twelve days to plod through the mud from his Virginia estate to the old City Hall in New York City to address the first session of Congress in 1789. Some members, living as far south as Georgia, needed another fortnight to make the trip by stagecoach.

Today, summoned by radio and using stratoliners, the 531 members of the 80th Congress could be assembled in Washington from the farthest corners of the nation in less than twelve hours. Those who happened to be in Europe or Asia would arrive a few hours later.

In 1789, Congress legislated for thirteen states with simple and not very dissimilar economies. Today, it must make laws applicable to forty-eight states, plus territories and possessions. The actual area involved has more than quadrupled. What is yet more significant is the wide difference in economic interests that range from the highly industrialized and densely populated large cities to the deserts of the Southwest, from the cranberry bogs of New England and the cottonfields of the South to the vast wheat farms of the Middle West and the wide-open spaces of the cattle-grazing prairies. The first national census, in 1790, recorded the population of the U.S.A. as a little under 4,000,000. In 1946, the Census Bureau says Americans number more than 139,000,000 souls, and the current birthrate is on the upgrade.

There was nothing in the trade statistics of that early era to cause the framers of the Constitution to imagine that some day the commerce clause they wrote would be the basis for more legislation and debate than any other phrase in the great national charter. The dollar value of American imports then was about $8,000,000 and exports ran about $20,000,000. Today, imports run into hundreds of millions and the U.S.A. is the leading exporter of the world. In 1943, excluding Lend-Lease and war supplies, the total was better than a billion dollars' worth of industrial products, The labor force swelled to more than 60,000,000 gainfully employed as America entered the year of 1946. National income reached a fantastic peak of 175 billion dollars.

Vast production has changed this nation from a not-very-important financial ward of Europe in the eighteenth century, to the leading creditor nation in all history. Financial missions from powers great and small knock at the Treasury for gifts and loans counted in billions.

In the First Congress twenty-six senators sat at desks which were equipped with snuffboxes. The snuffboxes still remain but there are now ninety-six senators. Hawaii and Alaska are asking for statehood, and there is always the intriguing possibility of Texas' dividing herself into four more states and sending eight more senators to Washington, as allowed for in her act of admission to the Union. Sixty-six men comprised the first House of Representatives; today, the clerk calls the roll for more than six times that many.

From 1787 to 1791 all revenues collected by the new national government amounted to less than $4,500,000. In 1945, Uncle Sam reached into the taxpayers' pockets for most of the $46,456,000,000 raised by the Treasury. On the expenditure side of the ledger, the comparison is even more fantastic, due in part to the war. Living within income, the federal expenditures for the first two years of Congress totalled only $4,261,000. In 1945, the Treasury was obligated to pay out more than $100,404,000,000. The most conservative balanced budgets envisioned for normal postwar years vary from twenty-five to thirty-five billion dollars.

In the first Washington administration, there were three small executive departments: State, Treasury, and War. The payrolls of that day, made out by hand, contained one hundred thirty-six names. Today, there are ten enormous departments—Justice, Post Office, Navy, Interior, Agriculture, Commerce, and Labor have been added in that order. There is constant pressure to enlarge this list.

There are today more than one hundred federal agencies, some of them, such as Federal Security and the Veterans Administration, as large as the cabinet departments. Intricate machines that duplicate the signature of a disbursing officer millions of times are needed to make out paychecks for the more than two million persons now on the federal payroll. That number decreases as war units are liquidated but there is no sign that Uncle Sam is in danger of losing his position as the largest employer in the country.

The First Congress passed just 118 laws, 108 public and 10 private. Most of those private laws were the result of claims against the government. The 79th Congress ground out 892 private bills, and added 734 public laws to the federal statute books.

The figures for other types of congressional action, such as the various kinds of resolutions, are even more remarkable. The total for the First Congress was sixteen. The 78th Congress passed 1690 resolutions, more than one hundred times as many.

In foreign relations, the change is not only startling but of the greatest significance for the future. Just one simple treaty was submitted to the Senate in the First Congress. There were twenty in the 79th, as well as nine international organization conventions. Congress is facing an entirely new series of difficult decisions in this area. It will take hundreds of international agreements, conventions, and treaties to adjust life among the nations of the world of tomorrow. International law is being rewritten to fit a much smaller world. Whereas most treaties until recently were made with a single country or only a few, Congress has already passed the United Nations Charter, the Bretton Woods monetary agreement, and enabling legislation for world aviation and world agricultural organizations. These instruments are open to adherence by many nations. Congress, including the House, which traditionally has no voice in treaty-making but should be a full partner in these deliberations, will have to devote more time to this broad field than ever before in its history.

We could go on indefinitely but the point is that, notwithstanding the vast expansion in every phase of our country's national and international life and especially in the growth of government in the past two decades, Congress, even with the recent improvements, has changed but little. The present legislative machinery was adequate for the political problems and relatively minor needs of commerce and industry in the infant years. There was ample time for debate and deliberation. Frequently discussions were continued in the evening in the spacious drawing room of some Washington mansion where one might have found a quorum of the Senate and House of that era.

Today, government is a labyrinth and the capabilities and energies of the five hundred thirty-one lawmakers are siphoned off into many non-legislative activities and dissipated by time-wasting trivia and archaic procedures. The comparisons sketched here tell in vivid fact and figure of the need in twentieth-century America for a complete modernization of congressional organization.

The Legislative Reorganization Act of 1946 is undoubtedly a step forward. Its sponsors, and the members of the 79th Congress, deserve much credit for what was done. But we believe sincerely that unless Congress is *further* strengthened and made more responsive to its added duties and functions, the time *could* come when American citizens might be tempted to forsake representative government. They might prefer a different nostrum—no doubt labeled "democracy" —which seemed to promise a more effective or more immediate solution to the issue that created the crisis.

CHAPTER 3

One Hundred Fifty-Eight Years of Tinkering

THERE IS A CONSTANT PARADOX IN AMERICAN NATIONAL LIFE
that is puzzling to sincere admirers in other lands of the
American way of getting things done. Along scientific and
material lines, the United States has outstripped every nation
on the face of the globe. But in its political institutions there
is a blind reverence for tradition that borders on idolatry.
Proponents of the 1946 changes in the national legislature
face the persistent argument that "the present organization
of Congress has worked well enough up to now so why
change it?" Enemies of progress can be counted upon to
oppose even more violently any further improvement.

Those who oppose any change often point to the cele-
brated "Hundred Days" in 1933 when dozens of measures
were placed on the statute books with record speed to rescue
the nation from its most serious depression. Likewise, they
point to World War II when all necessary legislation was
passed to enable the greatest of all trials by battle to be the
most efficiently fought. It sounds impressive, but let us take
a second look.

Is it to the credit of Congress that liaison with the Executive broke down so completely in the Hoover administration
as to produce a virtual deadlock in government? Or that

five hundred thirty-one representatives of people who were losing their savings, their homes, and even their faith in democracy, could produce no remedial legislation until the financial holocaust was upon the country, and once-self-sufficient men and women were begging for handouts?

Can Congress, as the great deliberative branch of government, take much glory even in the great achievements of the Roosevelt administration? Remember the grave days when a bill basically changing the nation's banking system shot through both houses with only a handful of the members of the House and Senate's having read it? President Roosevelt had gathered a galaxy of brilliant minds in his executive departments. Fortunately for Congress, these much-abused "bright young men" had the skill to turn out in quick succession many great pieces of legislation to accomplish, in some cases, long-overdue reforms. Legislators still burn with indignation at the "rubber stamp" label applied to Congress in those years. Could it be indignation born of frustration, because the legislative branch was not equipped to deal with the crisis?

The war record is good. Again, however, it was a lucky break, not a result of any regular procedure in the Senate or House, that then Senator Harry S. Truman got on the trail of waste and extravagance in military spending. The Truman committee, a special group and *not* a regularly functioning unit of the Congress, did a remarkable job in curbing recklessness. But even it sometimes reached the scene too late, as in the Canol oil project in the far north. Does anyone contend seriously that the Appropriations Committees with their tiny staffs were able to keep tab on the disbursal of the billions willingly voted to prosecute the war?

For instance, $40,000,000 was appropriated to build the famous Pentagon Building in Virginia, just across the Potomac River from Washington. This huge structure provided office space for nearly 40,000 War Department workers. And Congress set a limit of forty millions on its cost. As a result of a one-man investigation by Representative Albert J. Engel of Michigan, the actual, final cost of the Pentagon was discovered: $85,861,576. It is admitted that whatever millions were needed above the legal limit were obtained through some expert shuffling of funds by persons in the executive departments skilled at that sort of thing. The additional cost may have been justified completely, but the point is that Congress was unable to follow through adequately even on peacetime expenditures. This weakness became a glaring one as the war made it necessary to appropriate tens of billions, much of which had been loaned to the government by the public in the form of war bonds.

Has Congress been able to shape the proper tools sufficiently in advance to handle the difficult reconversion period? Does it have its own experts to help deal with surplus property disposal? Most members admit the first bill here was a sorry piece of law drafting. And what of housing, veterans' needs, liquidation of war agencies, the threat of inflation, labor unrest? Must it always trust to luck that the executive branch will produce the brains necessary to fashion good legislation to solve national issues as they arise?

Under the Reorganization Act, Congress now has additional staff for aiding its committees, which will enable it to do a better job. Unfortunately, the effectiveness of such staff will be greatly diminished by the failure of Congress to take its selection out of politics and put it under a civil service system to assure selection of personnel on merit only and to give them permanent tenure.

We raise these points as a prelude to proving that Congress in the past has not regarded its procedures as sacrosanct and that it has made many changes. The basic trouble has been that the alterations were too superficial. Complaints have been vocal and numerous. The result has been much as Mark Twain's observation about the weather.

Before the recent partial reorganization it was hard to understand why plans for revamping the committee lineup on Capitol Hill met such formidable opposition. It is natural for any chairman who might be affected, as well as the few directly in line to succeed him, to fight such proposals. No one likes to surrender a privilege or give up any power. But for the great majority, common sense should lead them to welcome a basic improvement. Neither the Senate nor the House has ever had any lasting regard for the number and functions of their committees.

Until Congress recently reduced them to thirty-four, there were almost a hundred committees, each with a chairman, a ranking minority member who would become chairman if his party came into power, and usually one or more clerks. The Senate had 33 regular and 9 special committees. The House had 48 regular and 6 specials. The combined total was ninety-six. Moreover, it was a rare week that did not see some member propose an addition to this lengthy list.

It will be helpful to take a quick glance at the evolution of this hodgepodge congressional system. It is a story of patchwork, improvisation, and tinkering for the one hundred fifty-eight years that Congress has been functioning.

Any new organization delegates groups of its members to handle certain functions. When the body is small, such groups are few and often temporary in nature; commonly, much of the business is transacted directly on the floor. So it was with the early Congresses. The development of committee responsibility and power was gradual in both chambers.

Let us look first at the Senate. In one brief span, 1815-1816, the Senate set up about one hundred special committees, but from its inception up to 1816, there were only four *regular* groups. Then came the first of several "major reorganizations." This one produced eleven standing committees where there had been four. Most of the special and temporary units were abolished.

Members were picked for committee posts by plurality vote with ballots. Initially, there were three senators on the average committee. That number expanded to seven by 1850, and by 1900 most regular units had nine members.

The number of committees increased gradually through the years and mounted to 74 by 1921. There became so many committee meetings that senators were prevented from attending floor sessions. There was much duplication and overlapping of functions. Then Senator Frank B. Brandegee of Connecticut precipitated another major shakeup; his resolution, passed in 1921, slashed the number of regular committees in half, to 34; it has now been cut to fifteen.

Among the prize exhibits of inefficiency exposed during the Brandegee fight were Indian Affairs and Appropriations. Four committees were working over the Indians, and no less than eleven claimed the duty of holding the purse-strings on what doubtless was called bureaucratic recklessness. The 1921 reorganization left one in each field.

There has since been no increase in the regular units. In the 80th Congress there are nineteen less yet even the number today keeps the lawmakers rushing from one meeting to another. A spectacular example was the coming-and-going of harassed members of the special Pearl Harbor Investigating Committee. One of the inevitable results, duplicated many times on both sides of the Capitol, was the repetitive questioning of important witnesses, with resultant delays, waste of time, and senseless piling up of the record, all at the taxpayers' expense. This condition was a factor in the blow-up which saw the distinguished counsel, William DeW. Mitchell, and his aides resign in disgust.

When members of both Senate and House sit on a single committee, it is called a joint committee. Such units are as old as Congress itself. With few exceptions, joint groups have been confined to handling ceremonial matters. One of these exceptions is the important device of the conference committee.

Whenever the two houses disagree upon a measure, and one chamber refuses to accept the other's version, a special group is selected to iron out the differences and work on the legislation until it is in language that both houses will approve. Both Senate and House must pass a bill in identical form, down to the last comma, before the measure goes to the President. A separate conference committee is formed each time these disagreements arise, and when the measure assigned to the group is disposed of, its work is ended. At any time there may be as many separate conference committees as there are disagreements between the two houses. This parliamentary device was set up in the opening weeks of the First Congress and continues unchanged to this day.

Other useful experiments in joint committees occurred in the period 1861-1872, growing out of the War Between The States. One such Senate-House group was set up to expedite the prosecution of the war shortly after the Union disaster at Ball's Bluff. This committee was more than a fly in Mr. Lincoln's ointment; the important principle in operation was Congress' taking positive action to examine the conduct of the Executive.

The Joint Select Committee on Retrenchment (1866-1872) was a second step in the same direction. Its work laid the foundations for the civil service system, and led to the gradual abatement of that obnoxious counterpart, the spoils system.

Nothing worries a politician more than the prospect of having to increase taxes. The temptation to reduce the federal "take" from the taxpayers' pockets is most understandable. Perhaps the high-tension political voltage involved caused Congress to put this important field of lawmaking on as high a professional plane as possible. In 1926 the Joint Committee on Internal Revenue Taxation was created, composed of ten members, five each from the regular committees handling tax matters—Senate Finance and House Ways and Means. The outstanding, modern feature of this move was the setting-up of a permanent, non-patronage, non-partisan staff of experts which works continuously the year round. Thus, one excellent group of professionals in tax matters serves both branches of Congress—a significant precedent.

There have been other attempts at reform aside from improving the committee structure. The Senate's zealously guarded right of unlimited debate is the most sacred cow on Capitol Hill. It is a privilege that leads to prostitution of the vital deliberative function and results in spectacular filibusters that at times have brought the entire legislative machinery of the Congress to a complete halt. As early as 1845, Daniel Webster attempted to remove Senator Hopkins L. Turney of Tennessee from the floor for "irrelevancy in debate." The move failed. In 1917, the Senate finally adopted a rule for the orderly ending of debate—cloture. However, because the upper chamber clings so tenaciously to its prerogative of freedom to talk about anything at any time, regardless of what issue may be before it, the cloture rule is seldom successfully invoked, and is almost a dead letter.

The Senate hit upon a useful aid in 1919 when the Legislative Drafting Service Act was passed, creating the Office of Legislative Counsel. The President of the Senate appoints lawyers who must be proficient in the art of writing good legislation. Committees have first call on the services of this group of law-drafting experts who, if they have any time left, also help individual senators.

Progress of a sort can likewise be recorded on the House side. For example, the House members now put their hats on racks in the lobby just off the chamber, as they would in any theatre or club. But for the first half-century, most of them wore their hats while attending to their lawmaking—a holdover from a more ancient day when parliaments used this custom to dramatize their independence of His Royal Majesty and his court prerogatives.

The committee system came about as gradually and as haphazardly in the House as in the Senate. In the early Congresses the practice was to thresh out details of a measure on the floor or appoint a special committee to study a bill. Hundreds of such committees were used.

The Louisiana Purchase (1803) led to the establishing of a permanent Public Lands Committee. The problem of acting as wet nurse and town council for the city of Washington early developed into a nuisance, so in 1808 the District of Columbia Committee became a fixed body. Special problems. usually taking the form of a demand from the public to remedy some evil allegedly existing in the executive branch. led to the formation of many committees. A regular unit to handle Executive Expenditures came in 1814. Six more committees to watch over various executive departments followed in 1816. Thus did much of the present House structure take shape more than a century ago.

There has been much tinkering through the years with the process of determining who shall vote the money. Under the Constitution, the House largely controls the federal purse-strings. It originates all appropriations and tax measures. To have a voice in deciding what bureau shall get how much is to possess a power useful in many ways. This is no innuendo. It is quite human for an executive unit to give the best possible service to any member who at least once a year is going to pass on the salaries and expenses of that bureau. Al Smith said: "You don't shoot Santa Claus," although the average bureaucrat is apt to feel, privately of course, that a member of the Appropriations Committee is a double for Scrooge.

Prior to 1865 the Ways and Means Committee handled both the outgo and the income, meaning appropriations and revenues. A new Appropriations Committee was set up that year; its power soon aroused jealousies. Open conflict erupted in 1880. Five years later the revolt became an uprising aimed primarily at the dictatorial procedures charged to the Appropriations Committee chairman, Samuel J. Randall. When the debate ended, there were eight independent appropriations units, one for each executive department.

This lineup survived the House upheaval of 1909-1911, and lasted until the 1921 Budget and Accounting Act, which folded the eight groups into the single Appropriations Committee of today. This body, the largest single committee in Congress, with 43 members, divides into 12 subcommittees of varying size, the largest having 11 members. They examine in detail the budgets of each executive department and agency, as well as the cash needs of Congress itself.

The House "revolution" of 1909-1911 was a spectacular battle. The rank and file, led by a young liberal from the West, George Norris of Nebraska, revolted against the almost legendary dictatorship of Speaker Joseph G. Cannon of Illinois, affectionately referred to as "Uncle Joe." If the even more important administrative issues of today were as simple and dramatic as they were then, American citizens would not be apathetic to modernizing Congress completely. By radio and in the press, the round-by-round accounts would be featured in top commentator spots and on the front page.

Radio forums would rival soap operas and comedians in their Hooper ratings.

The causes of the 1909-1911 revolt went back a long way. Almost every organization has an executive committee, and very early in its history the House created the Rules Committee; it had only five members. Likewise, every organization has a presiding officer; in the House, this is the Speaker. The stories of this committee and the office of the Speaker are closely linked.

Prior to 1841, things went along fairly quietly and the Rules group had no special privileges. But in that year it was granted authority to report "at all times," a favor accorded to no other committee. Then, in 1858, the Speaker became chairman of Rules, and the power of the committee was increased by giving priority to its reports. Since that day, the Speakership has been the key position in the House and the Rules Committee the most powerful group in his domain. From 1858 on, this combination began to run the House.

Twenty years later, the Rules group acquired the vital power of "special orders" by which it could control the order of business in the House. A majority of its members could force a bill to be taken up out of its regular place on the agenda, called "calendar" in the House. The Speaker also held the power of recognition of a member on the floor. Earlier decentralization of parliamentary power disappeared. The Speaker, both by virtue of his office and as head of the Rules Committee, acquired tremendous authority, and the office developed into the most powerful in all the government, next to the Presidency.

(Assertion of this power in the Hoover administration stirred up a social feud that rocked the teacups of the nation. Alice Roosevelt Longworth was the wife of the then Speaker Nicholas Longworth. She insisted that at all social functions, because her husband's position was second in importance only to that of the Chief Executive, she should outrank Dolly Gann, sister and hostess of the then Vice-President, Charles Curtis.)

The purpose of this "streamlining" was stated as enabling the majority to act quickly on legislation desired by the majority, and to override the minority whenever it attempted to obstruct business. The policy was embedded in the procedure of the House by the iron-handed rule of Speaker Thomas B. Reed of Maine and his Reed Rules of 1889.

The next step occurred in 1895 when the Rules Committee was given an even tighter grip on what bills would be allowed to come to a vote. Once again, the stated reason was to prevent filibustering or endless talk aimed at obstruction and delay. The "will of the majority," however, deteriorated into the wishes of just three men. The Speaker was chairman and picked two members from his party, thus gaining control in the little group of five. This trio determined all actions of the committee and therefore governed the House. The other two members, selected by the minority party, could only make futile gestures.

The policies of Uncle Joe Cannon fitted into this scheme like a glove on a woman's hand. Uncle Joe served forty-six years in the House before retiring in March, 1923, at the age of eighty-six. Stories about him could fill a separate volume. A group of members once protested that the Speaker and his two cohorts on the Rules Committee were thwarting the will of the people because they didn't keep their ears to the ground to learn what the people wanted. Replied Cannon:

"Some Congressmen keep their ear so close to the ground that they get both ears on the ground. Only two other animals can do that—a donkey and a jack rabbit."

By 1909, the Speaker's power and that of his Rules Committee had become more than most members could stand.

Cannon appointed all the committees and named their chairmen. The penalty of insurgency—and Uncle Joe was the judge of what constituted insurgency—was poor committee appointments, failure to recognize those who protested, and loss of patronage. Blind and servile party loyalty became the only way to advancement in the House.

Young Representative Norris broke many a lance against this combination. Finally, in the years 1909 and 1911, he led the membership in a successful revolt against Cannonism. When it was over, here is what had happened.

Speaker Cannon and his successors were stripped of three mighty props to their dictatorship. The Speaker was deprived of his membership on the Rules Committee. His absolute power of recognition was abolished. The appointment of committees was taken from him and lodged with the House.

Actually, this meant selection by party caucus, and Uncle Joe dominated that for some time. However, he was succeeded in 1911 by Champ Clark of Missouri, and the power of the Rules Committee was further curbed when the House voted that any bill had to be on the House calendar for at least three days before it could be brought to a vote. Other procedural changes were made to ensure greater legislative freedom, and six superfluous committees were abolished.

In 1915 the House devised its own research aid by creating the Legislative Reference Service of the Library of Congress, which worked well on a limited scale until the Legislative Reorganization Act of 1946, when it was finally provided with adequate funds to enable it to hire a first-class, professionally trained staff commensurate with its grave responsibilities to Congress. The joint tax group was formed in 1926 as previously noted. In 1927 another reorganization was put through by the Republicans: sixteen more-or-less dormant expenditure committees were abolished. The changes were not fundamental, however. From that date until the Reganization Act, only minor alterations were made.

This brief summary shows that both the Senate and House have been changing their rules and procedures continuously. Most of these changes have been expedients to meet particular situations which developed from time to time. The exceptions were the great fight to free the House of an intolerable dictatorship that developed at the turn of the century, and the reorganization of 1946. However, there still remain undemocratic procedures which urgently need correction.

This review of the history of legislative reorganization proves that a thorough overhauling of the congressional machinery will shatter no precious precedents. We turn now to the positive side of this study, dealing first with that phase of Congress best known to the public—the transaction of the public's business on the floors of the Senate and House. By statute, the La Follette-Monroney committee was barred from considering any changes in this field, but members testified before that group as to the vital need for improvement in floor procedures if Congress is to regain prestige and power.

CHAPTER 4

They Come, They See — And Are Disappointed

THE NATIONAL CAPITAL IS AN INCREASINGLY IMPORTANT rival of New York City, California, Niagara Falls, and Florida as a tourist mecca. By 1940 the annual influx of visitors had reached approximately four million. Now they are coming again, in even greater numbers. These men, women, and children are a wonderful cross-section of the United States. What is important to Congress is that for tens of thousands, especially the young students from public and private schools who pour in, shepherded by their instructors, there is something more than recreation, scenic beauty, and historic shrines that brings them to Washington from the cities and crossroads. They want to see their great national government at work. They want to see Congress.

These future voters crowd through the public portions of the White House, they see money made at the Bureau of Engraving and Printing, they are fingerprinted at FBI Headquarters, they gaze in awe at the stately decor of the Supreme Court, and in wonder at the colossal Pentagon Building. And they come to Capitol Hill to see the Senate and House making laws for the nation. For most, the only previous tangible impression they have had of Congress has come through exciting broadcast, newsreel, or press accounts of an opening day or of a President addressing a joint session.

They go to the Senate. There they may see a great argument on a vital international issue suddenly interrupted by a senator who will proceed to make a long speech that has no bearing at all on the subject being debated. They may see a senator making a speech to an almost empty chamber. They may see his colleagues reading newspapers or just wandering in and out.

They go to the House. And there they may see less than ten per cent of the 435 members on the floor. They may see a chamber filled with milling, talking members rushing about while a clerk, calling the roll, intones names for forty-five minutes. They may see a congressman speaking earnestly in the "well" of the House while his fellow members engage in amiable conversation all over the place and bob in and out at the rear of the chamber where (a guide tells them) the cloakrooms are located.

Talk to any of these boys and girls after such an experience. We have. One reaction is almost invariable—disappointment. And for many there is something more dangerous—disillusionment. This is not to contend that Congress can order its business so as to produce, every day, an exciting, historic drama, a show that could compete in listener interest with network radio programs or in reader interest with the story that gets the eight-column headline. But it should spur thoughtful members to demand a searching inquiry into the present procedures on the floor of both the Senate and the House.

To get a better perspective, let us consider the original conceptions of the two Houses. The difference in size—96 senators against 435 representatives—which exists today, is no accident. Among the members of the Constitutional Convention of 1787 there was a genuine fear of democracy. Due to property qualifications, most of the so-called "common" people were disfranchised. The upper classes hoped to keep things that way. Senator Elbridge Gerry of Massachusetts summarized this distrust and contempt for the masses when he said: "The evils we experience flow from the excess of Democracy. The people do not lack virtue but are the dupes of 'pretended patriots.'" In 1946, Senator Millard Tydings of Maryland said on the floor, during a filibuster to prevent consideration of a bill to establish a Fair Employment Practices Commission: "The rule of majority, the rule of votes. Majority to hades. . . ."

The evidence in the early record forces us to agree with the conclusion reached in such historical studies as those of Charles A. Beard and J. Allen Smith, namely, that the conservative founders desired to establish an exclusive sort of rich man's club in the Senate, as far removed as possible from the "people." By and large, they succeeded. Despite its fairly recent democratization, the Senate still has a definite, albeit charming, clubbiness that reveals itself in many small customs and in the extreme lengths to which senatorial courtesies are carried. The exception to this generalization is that today not as many senators would be classified as wealthy as was formerly the case.

The Constitution-makers decided a senator would serve in office six years, in contrast to the short two-year term of a representative in the House. The popular "lower" chamber —and it was considered an inferior body—was planned as a large debating society, subject to complete turnover of all its members every two years. A turbulent and somewhat irresponsible House was envisioned. There are occasions when this prediction is fulfilled.

The Senate was to be the stable representative of the propertied group which dominated colonial America. The initial requisites for election to that body make this abundantly clear. Senators were to be selected by the respective state legislatures. It was considered most unlikely that any man would be chosen unless he possessed substantial means. Election of most state legislators at that time rested on property ownership. A large majority of the people possessed no such tangible assets and therefore could not participate even in their state governments. Accordingly, senators were chosen by the wealthier conservative classes, and most of the people had little voice in the matter.

Equally important, the artisans of the national charter wanted to assure continuity in office of this conservative group. So they had the Constitution provide that only one-third of the Senate was to be up for election every two years. This meant that there would always be a carryover of two-thirds; the provision was designed to assure a conservative majority at all times. And although property qualifications for voting gradually disappeared in the states, this system of choosing members of the Senate survived all attempts to change it for more than a century.

The more democratic method of the direct primary and popular election of senators was achieved with the Seventeenth Amendment to the Constitution, which became effective in 1913. With liberalized qualifications for voting and holding office, the aristocratic Senate, originally designed as a bulwark for those who today would be said to belong in the "high income tax brackets," gradually came to be a popular forum for a few bold representatives of the people. However, the provision for election of only one-third of the Senate every two years remains. Accordingly, there still is a lag between constitutional machinery and the political facts.

This obvious check on the people as represented by the House became an anachronism once these same people also elected senators. While the people needed a check upon the arbitrary actions of kings and despots, which was the function of the first parliaments, assuredly in a democracy they should not need a check upon themselves.

We believe the two great branches of the national legislature should be placed on a more equal footing, not because of the real or imagined disparagement in prestige, but on the grounds of efficiency. The term of a representative should be extended so that a House member may "get his feet wet" before having to seek reelection. The present period of two years hardly gives him time to begin his public duties before he has to prepare for the next primary. Some districts change their representative at almost every election. The constituents of such districts suffer as a result. No new member of the House can acquire much influence or accomplish a great deal in a single twenty-four-month span of office, whereas a senator has time and opportunities to get his legislative proposals enacted into law. Therefore, we agree entirely with Representative Lowell Stockman of Oregon and many others who advocate a four-year term for members of the House.

There is a strong case for abolishing the present exclusive right of the Senate to handle treaties, which will be presented later. This, the equalizing of tenure of office, and the giving to residents in the District of Columbia of representation in Congress, would require constitutional amendments. Of all the suggestions to be made in this volume these are the only three that require such action. We believe these changes are important enough to an efficient democracy to justify that effort.

Both Senate and House normally meet at noon, Monday through Friday, and are opened with prayers by chaplains who are regular employees. The record of the legislative action of the preceding session is read, but from this point on the floor practices of the two bodies diverge sharply.

One of the most discouraging problems that confronts students of government in this country is the slow manner in which the Senate sometimes functions. It results in many instances in delaying unconscionably or stalling completely a decision on important legislation. We refer to the practically unlimited speaking and debating privileges on the Senate floor. The popular description of the Senate as the "world's greatest deliberative body" becomes a farce and mockery as abuse of these privileges goes unchecked session after session.

Slavish devotion to this tradition of unlimited debate led the Senate to restrict the power of the Joint Committee on the Organization of Congress. The vast majority in both houses recognized the need for getting recommendations that could form the basis of legislation to convert Congress into a modern instrument of the people. But the Senate would take no chances on even an advisory finding that might reflect on its present eighteenth-century floor procedure. Accordingly, at its insistence, the following language was put in the measure creating the Joint Committee:

". . . Provided that nothing in this concurrent resolution shall be construed to authorize the committee to make any recommendations with respect to the rules, parliamentary procedure, practices and/or the precedents of either House, or the consideration of any matter on the floor of either House. . . ." The effect of this prohibition was to tell the La Follette-Monroney committee not to tamper with the Senate's sacred cow—the right to filibuster.

We doubt if there ever lived a member of any legislative body who did not at some time feel that a measure about to be enacted was the worst possible course of action that could be taken. A legislator uses every parliamentary means available to gain time to line up votes for his side through explanation in debate and personal persuasion. If his efforts fail, he has done his duty and accepts the will of the majority. That is the essence of democracy at work. To protect individuals and minorities against excesses of the majority there are those "certain inalienable rights" in the Constitution, and a Supreme Court to strike down legislation that trespasses them. The Senate rules, however, operate as if there were no Constitution or Supreme Court.

A small group, sometimes a single senator, opposes a bill known to be favored by an overwhelming majority. It may have already passed the House by a wide margin. This small minority plans deliberately to prevent the Senate from ever voting on the measure. One of their number gets control of the floor. This can be obtained on as flimsy a point as correcting the grammar in the prayer uttered by the Senate chaplain on the previous day—as was done in January, 1946, by Senator John Overton of Louisiana.

Once in control, so long as the "debate" continues the Senate cannot take a single legislative action except by the grace of those who, under its own rule, are now its masters. The presiding officer is powerless, the majority almost so. When this utter negation of democratic procedure is in progress, there exists the parliamentary farce called a filibuster. The power of the filibusterers lies in their ability to hold up all pending legislation, no matter how vital it may be to the nation, until the majority knuckles under and agrees to their point. That point usually is to kill the bill they are opposing although, under Senate rules, not a word need be said directly about the measure during the entire "debate."

This fantastic extension of senatorial courtesies has been called legislative piracy, and whoever termed the device a filibuster doubtless had in mind the origins of that word. The Dutch *vrijbuiter*, meaning freebooter, was applied by the English to seventeenth-century buccaneers who plundered Spanish ships in the Caribbean. The Spanish called the same pirates *filibusteros*. *Filibuster* later came to embrace illegal expeditions of international adventurers against the sovereignty of a group or nation for personal gain. Now the word aptly denotes legislative freebooting and buccaneering, with this important exception—in the Senate, it is all very legal.

A cursory review of measures killed by filibusters does not support the view that the participants are always battling courageously against mob rule. A particular anti-monopoly law may be of doubtful constitutionality. It may be impractical of enforcement. But when a few men prevent an overwhelming majority of the House and Senate from giving such a law a fair test, the unctuous arguments about protecting the nation against the excesses of a majority become ridiculous.

How does a filibuster keep going? From the moment a senator rises to his feet and is recognized by the presiding officer, he may talk as long as his voice and lungs hold out and he may discuss any topic he wishes without any regard to the legislation that is under consideration. One-man filibusters are the most spectacular. In June, 1935, Huey Long spoke from 12:15 P.M. one afternoon until 3:15 A.M. the next morning, fifteen hours, with only one quorum call to give him a ten-minute rest. The Louisiana dictator, gesturing wildly and speaking in that hoarse, raspy voice that held many listeners spellbound, entertained with Creole stories, orated several hours on the fine art of making his favorite dish, potlikker, read the Bible, and put on a crowd-pleasing show. He was on his feet the entire fifteen hours.

Another famous one-man filibuster was staged by Senator Robert La Follette, Sr., back in 1908, when he held the Senate in session continuously for almost two days in a battle against the Aldrich-Vreeland currency bill. However, a quorum in the Senate is one-half of all the members plus one, and the elder La Follette was aided by more than thirty roll calls during his filibuster. He had his secretary give him a signal when less than a quorum was on the floor and then would automatically get a breathing spell by demanding a roll call.

When the leader of a filibuster has a group of colleagues supporting him, it is relatively easy to keep the Senate stalled indefinitely by this quorum device, and by the simple ruse of yielding to a friendly speaker who will then consume several hours with his "interruption."

One way to break up a filibuster is for the majority to organize, keep a quorum in the chamber, and refuse to adjourn, thus holding the Senate in continuous session until the filibusterers are exhausted physically. Once, in 1915, in a battle over a rivers and harbors bill, the Senate sat from noon Monday until 6 P.M. Wednesday, fifty-four hours, but even then it was the majority that finally surrendered and the filibuster which was successful. Of late, the majority seems to have had no stomach for such legislative marathons. They are a real menace to the health of the members.

The 1915 filibuster lasted thirty-two days. That same year there occurred another one of twenty-three days against a ship purchase bill. Thus the two consumed fifty-five days, more than two months of the session. The preceding year, the Senate had endured a twenty-one-day filibuster against anti-trust legislation, and in 1890 there was one against the "Force Bill," an election law, that took up a month of the upper body's time. The longest filibuster on record occurred in 1893, against repeal of a silver purchase law. It consumed forty-six business days.

The experiences of 1914-15 led to agitation for correction of this abuse that perverts the legislative process, and the result was the adoption by the Senate, on March 8, 1917, of the standing rule of cloture. It operates this way:

When eighteen or more senators file a petition to invoke the cloture rule, a vote automatically is taken after one day has intervened. If two-thirds of the senators present favor cloture (there must, of course, be a quorum), then the bill the filibuster was seeking to block must come to a vote. Theoretically, each of the ninety-six senators is allowed to use up to one hour's time after the rule limiting debate has been adopted. In practice, adoption of cloture usually is followed immediately by a vote on the measure that has been awaiting a decision.

Seventeen times between 1917 and 1946 the majority has tried to invoke cloture but the move has succeeded in only four instances, two of them historic. In November, 1919, the dilatory opposition of the "little band of irreconcilables" led by Senator Henry Cabot Lodge of Massachusetts was broken, and the Senate voted on the Treaty of Versailles. Likewise, the filibuster of Senator Irvine L. Lenroot of Wisconsin was stamped out by cloture in March, 1926, and the World Court issue came to a vote. Twice in quick succession, in 1927, the rule was used to permit a roll call on amendments to the National Banking Act and a decision on the proposal of Senator Wesley L. Jones of Washington to create a Prohibition Bureau.

The necessary two-thirds vote for cloture could not be obtained in the dozen other cases, which included unsuccessful attempts to end filibusters against the Colorado River development, tariff amendments, anti-lynch and anti-poll tax proposals, and the eighteen-day filibuster in 1946 against the Fair Employment Practices Commission.

Why does cloture fail so often? Why do senators time and again vote against invoking the rule that would end a filibuster, even when they favor the bill the minority seeks to kill? The conclusion seems inescapable that they cherish this arbitrary power that lies in every senator's hand, feeling they may sometime wish to filibuster themselves against a measure they oppose. It's a form of senatorial courtesy or, less elegantly: "You scratch my back and I'll scratch yours."

In addition to those mentioned above, a number of petitions to shut off debate have been started but dropped or withdrawn when the odds appeared hopeless or a compromise was worked out. Equally harmful is the effect of the mere threat of a filibuster. Administration leaders, particularly toward the end of a crowded session, sometimes are forced to make concessions wholly unwarranted on any basis of merit to avoid having the Senate tied up in a knot by a filibuster with the risk of important measures failing to get action.

The problem is to devise a practical cloture rule that will guarantee every senator the right to present his views fully on any given legislative issue, but which will end the abuse of the debate privilege which exposes the entire legislative branch of the government to the contempt of American people and to international ridicule. A simple solution would be to amend the present rule so that unlimited debate would end automatically when a majority of the entire Senate signed a petition to invoke cloture.

On the House side, the situation is reversed. The member's problem there is to figure out how to get a chance to speak at a time when enough members will be around to make it worthwhile. Legislative days in the so-called lower chamber are planned ahead, often for a week in advance. Because of the large membership, it takes longer to transact routine business. Debate has to be circumscribed. Party considerations, personal prejudices, and unrelated political controls sometimes are determining factors. The Speaker and the

House Rules Committee are powerful forces in the supervision of debate.

Certain days are set aside every week for consideration of various types of bills. With nineteen regular committees now working over the thousands of measures introduced, a backlog accumulates early in the session. The Rules Committee supposedly is not a legislative unit but a traffic policeman who sees that important issues get a green light to proceed to the floor. However, there is an unchecked tendency of this powerful group to act as judge and jury on the merits of legislation ready to be considered by the House. It attempts to force changes in bills to suit the predilections of a majority of its members. In one instance, it even substituted another measure, the Case labor bill in 1946, for the one that the House Labor Committee had reported out for consideration, thus usurping the function of a regular legislative committee.

As its name implies, the Rules Committee brings in a rule which specifies how much time will be allowed for debate on the bill that is to be taken up. On occasion, it also prescribes the exact parliamentary method to be used in handling the measure. Sometimes the House feels that it is being gagged and liberalizes the rule before adopting it. The vote on adopting the rule is a test of strength between opposing forces and frequently foreshadows the final vote on the issue, which may be several days distant. When the bill itself is taken up, the Democrats and Republicans divide the allotted time evenly, and leaders of the respective parties assigned to supervise the debate parcel out so many minutes to this and that member seeking time. When the amendment stage is reached, each member can have five minutes to speak on the amendment then being considered. But here is the important factor: *All debate must be germane to the matter*

before the House. This avoids the abuse of debate that prevails in the Senate.

Members have indirect ways of getting the floor. When a congressman thinks he has been attacked personally, he states his case briefly. If the Speaker agrees, he is allowed an hour on a "point of personal privilege" to air his grievance. Clever parliamentarians use this and other devices to make speeches. Generally, however, there are only two times that one has an opportunity to address his fellow members.

At the opening of each session, after the journal is read and before proceeding to the calendar of the day, there is an interval when a member may get unanimous consent to speak for one minute. If the House is tolerant that particular morning, he may get five minutes to say his piece. He can also take the minute and then get permission to "extend my remarks in the *Record* at this point." So, the next day, in the *Congressional Record*—that daily verbatim transcript of the proceedings of Congress—it will appear to the unknowing reader as if the member had made a full-dress speech to the House. The other chance to speak is to obtain time at the close of the day's business. Then a member talks largely to empty benches and tired pageboys.

We propose that daily time should be set aside for members to speak on bills they have introduced and in which they are particularly interested. This right to speak should be automatic, depending on the date such request is made and the first allotted time that is available. Thirty minutes to an hour immediately following the regular legislative program could be used very profitably for these speeches. Many may think such a suggestion fantastic in view of the present crowded schedule of the House. But we intend to show how at least thirty-five days in an average session could be saved by adopting thorough streamlining procedures. If this were done, time could be well spent in making the House a more deliberative body than it is under present conditions.

Another practice that exposes Congress to valid criticism and creates antagonism between the executive and legislative branches is the subterfuge of adding an irrelevant amendment to an important bill. This addition actually may be a complete bill dealing with a subject totally unrelated to the legislation of which it becomes a part. Such amendments are popularly and aptly called "riders."

The Senate, throughout the years, has been more guilty in this matter than the House, for in the latter body an amendment that is not germane to the bill may be thrown out, generally under the rules, if a point of order is made against it. However, riders *have* been added in the House. In fact, the Rules Committee can and has, in deciding how a measure shall be brought to a vote, actually encouraged riders by nullifying the rule of germaneness.

In years past most riders appeared attached to appropriation bills in the Senate. The Senate took cognizance of this unhealthy practice by amending its rules so as to prohibit it in the Reorganization Act of 1946. However, the real evil still remains because riders to measures other than appropriation bills have not been outlawed. It is therefore essential that we consider the reasons for prohibiting riders to *any* bills, whether added in the House or the Senate.

The Constitution contemplates that controversial issues will be considered and met on their merits and not included as a part of a bill to which they have no relevancy. The basic law places this responsibility upon Congress, and it anticipates that the President will have the opportunity of considering measures separately when determining whether to use his veto power.

Sponsors of riders betray their weakness when they resort

to this device of tacking pet schemes onto the backs of stronger legislation. The reason appropriation bills were the favorite victims of this parasitic process was because the operations of a major government department are crippled unless its budget measure becomes law by July 1st of each year, the beginning of the new fiscal year. The President would thus hesitate to veto a necessary bill because of the calamity that might result if he did, and the rider usually got by.

Many Presidents have spoken out in just anger at Capitol Hill when forced to accept riders. The 79th Congress passed an appropriation bill rescinding the authority to spend billions of dollars that had been voted while the war still was in progress. The White House thoroughly approved this move to readjust executive finances to the postwar reconversion period. Written into the measure, however, there was in effect a separate bill to break up the national system of employment offices, the United States Employment Service, into fifty-one separate state and territorial systems. Vetoing the entire bill in December, 1945, President Harry Truman said forcefully:

"It seems clear to me that a matter of such grave importance as our public employment system deserves not only permanent legislation, but legislation carefully and separately considered. Issues of such a difficult and vital nature should not be dealt with as riders to appropriation bills. . . . To attach a legislative rider to an appropriation bill restricts the President's exercise of his functions and is contrary to good government. . . . It has long been considered a fundamental principle that legislation on a major issue of policy ought not to be combined with an appropriation measure. The present bill directly violates that principle. I am obliged to withhold my approval to some very excellent legislation because of the objectionable practice which has been followed in attaching this rider which I cannot possibly approve."

Riders began to appear as early as 1855, when a tariff bill was added to a regular budget measure. In 1913, a rider on a money bill specified that none of the appropriation allowed for enforcing the Sherman anti-trust act could be used to prosecute farmers' societies or labor unions. An Indian Bureau appropriation once contained detailed provisions for suppressing traffic in liquor among the braves, regulation of mining, and authority to investigate the conduct of the Indian Service.

District of Columbia budget bills are favorite victims. One rider provided for revoking licenses of secondhand dealers when they purchased stolen pipe. Nationwide in its effect was the District bill rider containing the basic law around which was built the so-called Fair Trade Act in forty-five states. President Roosevelt protested vigorously that this was class legislation but had to sign the entire bill rather than stall the operation of the municipal government of Washington.

How is the House going to cut down its work so that those fifty days we mentioned can be employed more usefully than at present? In the first place, abolish the House District Committee and more than thirteen valuable legislative days will be salvaged.

Every other Monday is set aside for District of Columbia legislation. Under a strict interpretation of the Constitution, Congress since 1878 has denied local self-government to the many people residing in the sixty-three square miles comprising the District of Columbia and completely occupied by the city of Washington. Today they number nearly a million voteless citizens. As a result, all local ordinances, such as a city council should consider, have to go through Congress in the same manner as important national legislation. The District of Columbia Committees in the Senate and House handle this chore.

On these Mondays one finds congressmen, in session assembled, acting as town councilmen and arguing over issues like the number of taxicabs to be licensed or the reinstatement of policemen fired from the local force. These trivia produce lengthy and heated debate. The penchant of a national legislator to act at times like a spoiled child is painfully exposed. Members rant churlishly over an alleged insult to their dignity by a local official, or by city residents. The colorful former Senator Coleman L. Blease of South Carolina once made a speech because he wasn't given a seat in a crowded streetcar.

The Legislative Reorganization Act attempted to handle another evil that formerly took so much of Congress' time. private claims against the government. It provided for the new Federal Tort Claims Act. Under this act, claims for $1000 or less can be settled by the federal agency concerned, while larger amounts are to be handled by the federal courts. This is undoubtedly a fine method of relieving Congress of a trivial, time-consuming task so that it can attend to the nation's important legislative business. But too many legalistic hands appear to have prepared the act, and we fear its limited scope and legalistic exceptions may result in having many private claim problems still thrown into the fully occupied lap of Congress.

Should one be surprised, therefore, if young future voters go home with a cynical estimate of their Congress, if they happen to go into the House galleries when purely local and strictly private matters are being discussed on the floor? This is not criticism of a hardworking group. Members of Congress didn't seek such thankless and irritating assignments. It is an indictment of an outworn system. Transfer these functions to a responsible local government and the job will be done much better. The House will gain many precious hours on the floor for matters properly of national concern. The Senate usually takes less time for this class of legislation but even there the saving would be considerable.

The next step in conserving time and energy of members of both houses is so important, and the results possible from its adoption so startling, that we have given it a separate chapter. It involves the use of mechanized voting.

CHAPTER 5

Voting by Electricity

————————————

MECHANIZED VOTING IS AN EASY, PRACTICAL, AND ALMOST obvious solution to the greatest single waste of time on Capitol Hill. Hours and hours are consumed at every session of Congress in calling the roll in the respective chambers. Naturally the problem is about four times as acute in the House as in the Senate because of the difference in numbers. The Senate clerks usually go through their list of 96 names in about ten minutes. But calling off the 435 names in the House, then doing a repeat for members not responding, added to the curious little show put on in front of the Speaker's table after upward of 40 minutes have elapsed, when panting members just arrived on the floor are trying to get on the record by convincing the presiding officer that they didn't hear their names called or were unavoidably detained until the last moment—all this requires three-quarters of an hour every time a member makes a point of no quorum, unless the House chooses to adjourn.

Recorded votes are very necessary because the people have a right to know how each member votes on each issue brought to a decision in Congress. But in the House, this necessary function is perverted into a form of filibustering that frequently can consume hours. During the 79th Congress the House wasted several days answering roll calls. During these days no business was transacted. Usually such roll-call tactics are successful because less than a quorum stays in the chamber as the debate drags on. This does not necessarily reflect a lack of interest in the question up for discussion. It is the pressure of other work, the mail, telephone calls, visitors, and other aspects of the "Washington Representative" business that forces members to be absent from the floor. Here is an illustration that occurs often enough to condemn the present antiquated system of oral roll calls.

When the bells sound throughout the corridors of the office buildings, the committee rooms, and the restaurants of the Capitol, a House member can figure he has at least a half-hour to dictate a few more letters, make a few more phone calls to different departments, finish his already delayed lunch, or conclude a discussion on some point being considered in a committee. So he waits until the last warning bell, then streaks through the subways, arrives breathless at the entrance to the chamber, asks the doorkeeper what the vote is about, snags a fellow member to inquire "which way are we voting on this?", and then dashes onto the floor just under the wire to put himself on record.

Members may even be visiting some department downtown, having left word with their office where to reach them. The secretary calls to say a vote is on. The member grabs his hat, dashes for the nearest exit to find a cab and get back to the "Hill" in time to be recorded. One member of the 80th Congress, the amiable Lansdale Sasscer of nearby Maryland, confides that he has, on occasion, been able to race all the way to the chamber from his home at Upper Marlboro, nineteen miles from Washington, in time to beat the final rap of the Speaker's gavel closing the voting.

It's different in the Senate. There members start for the

floor as soon as they hear the gongs in the office or corridors. They get an elevator instantly by pushing the button three times, and have the luxury of covering the quarter of a mile underground via the ancient but remarkably efficient little monorail open-seat subway car that never ceases to intrigue visitors, young and old.

Here is a graphic summary of the staggering waste of time involved in the present laborious and tedious oral roll-call method:

	Number of Roll Calls			Hours Consumed	Legislative
	1943	*1944*	*1945*	(3-year Average)	Days Consumed [1]
HOUSE	174	126	187	121.8	24.3
SENATE	647	325	328	79.5	15.9

Except toward the end of a session, both houses meet only five days a week, so this table means that in the past three years the House alone required ONE ENTIRE LEGISLATIVE MONTH IN EACH YEAR *just for roll calls*. The Senate consumed sixty per cent as much. Of all the antiquated procedures on Capitol Hill, this one undoubtedly pulls down the efficiency of Congress more than any other single practice.

The remedy is simple—recording votes electrically. It has been tested over a period of thirty years beginning in the Wisconsin legislature in 1917, and is used regularly today in eleven state legislatures, including both houses of conservative Virginia. Several other states are considering its installation. Yet the proposal always encounters formidable opposition at the Capitol, particularly from colleagues in the House.

Perhaps they have been alarmed at the speed that Texans claim for their voting machines. A report from Austin says

---

[1] The typical legislative day, averaged over a period of years, runs from noon to 5 P.M.—a total of five hours.

they can vote the entire state house membership of 150 in
21 seconds, and on one occasion took 30 complete votes in
as many minutes. More likely, House members suffer from
the inertia toward change that afflicts most people. Although
senators have had regularly assigned desks for years, congressmen wander around at will and use any convenient seat so
long as it is on the side of the center aisle designated for their
party. This ancient custom is quite informal and comfortable, and would have to be relinquished in order to introduce mechanized voting. The electric vote recorder requires
that legislators be given regular places; an arm of each seat
contains the electric plugs for registering votes, and can be
used only when an individual key is inserted.

However, the advantages are so overwhelming that we propose that the following system be used in both houses to
replace the cumbersome calling of names by tally clerks
whose vocal stamina is amazing. The Senate quorum would
remain unchanged. In the House, 100 members would constitute a quorum at all times. When the "ayes and nays"
were ordered, the bells would ring as they do now. But there
would follow an automatic recess of from five to eight minutes which would give the members time to get to the floor.
During this interval, the tally clerks would insert the official
tally sheet and the necessary copies for use by the official
reporters and the radio and press galleries. This sheet would
contain the name, party, and state of every member of the
Senate or House.

At the expiration of the five- to eight-minute recess, the
chamber would come to order. The clerk would report that
the machine was ready to record the vote, and, at a sign from
the presiding officer, would push the button activating the
entire machine. The presiding officer might say something to
the effect that "the members will now vote." Each member
would then vote yes or no by inserting his key in the proper

slot on the arm-rest of his assigned seat. He would vote green for "yes" and red for "no." These lights would then flash, and remain on beside his name on the large wall chart in front of the chamber.

The machine would record how the member voted the instant he inserted his key, by perforating "yes" or "no" beside his name on the tally sheet. If a member had made a mistake (the lights would still be on so he could make a personal check), he would ask for permission from the chair to change his vote, just as he does now. The tally clerk would hand the final official sheet to the presiding officer, who would then announce the vote, push the "off" button, the lights would go out, and the vote would be completed.

The presiding officer might continue to announce "pairs" as is done now. An overly simple explanation of pairs is that when a member knows he will miss a roll call, he may report in advance how he would have voted if able to be present. His intention is matched with someone similarly absent who would have cast an opposite vote, and their names are paired in the *Congressional Record,* for the information of colleagues and constituents.

It takes more time to spell out this mechanized procedure than would be required for the actual voting. Adoption of the automatic recess admittedly would mean that not as much time would be saved in the Senate as in the House, but in a fast roll call the electric voting machine reduces the possibility of error, and it certainly is more efficient than the present method. Employing it, the Senate would still save eight days in an ordinary session.

In the House, we estimate the entire time for voting electrically, including the recess, would be from ten to twelve minutes, thus saving a full half-hour on every roll call. The accuracy would be unchallenged. At present, with the hubbub created by members coming in late and the hum of conversation that usually prevails, it is surprising that the tally clerks make as few errors as they do.

The ancient practice of the "teller vote" could also be abolished. Its purpose originally was to save time and still get a reasonably close count. It functions this way: The members leave their seats and congregate in the well of the House, then pass in single file up the center aisle to be counted by a supporter on each side of the question at issue. It takes about ten minutes. The weakness of the teller vote method is that the individual member is not recorded and usually only a small portion of the entire membership participates.

There have been occasions when its historic use was distorted, when teller votes were used in order to get an accurate count, and also to enable members to avoid having their votes recorded. This charge was made freely in the historic utility battle of a few years ago. The House Rules Committee brought in a special order permitting "only" a teller vote on the crucial "death sentence" clause in the Public Utilities Holding Company bill. Furious at this maneuver, the Scripps-Howard newspapers, who were supporting the measure, decided to try and record a teller vote for the first time in the history of Congress, and thus put members squarely on record who allegedly were dodging the issue. Interest in this daring journalistic counterattack was second only to the outcome of the vote. On the Scripps-Howard staff at the time was a young reporter with an unusual memory for names and faces. While members, gathering in the well to pass by the tellers, either smiled encouragement or shook their fists at the press gallery, the reporter coolly called off 286 of them to four other staffers who recorded the names and passed them to other reporters at telephones. The Scripps-Howard paper was on the street in forty minutes with a tally of names that subsequently proved to contain only one error.

Mechanical voting would eliminate that kind of abuse of the teller vote. Its real purpose—to save time—would be bettered and there would be more accuracy. And those young gallery visitors—we think they are very important—certainly would get a businesslike impression of the House at work. It is an example of where efficiency would focus more favorable attention on Congress.

We believe sincerely that the suggestions pertaining to filibusters and mechanical voting will enhance greatly the prestige of Congress and accomplish much in making the Senate and House more efficient. However, adoption of all or part of the suggestions made up to this point still would not remedy one grave defect in the present system of checks and balances between the executive and the legislative branches, which has been said to have degenerated into "more checks than balances." Ways must be found to achieve closer coordination between these two branches of the government, and we turn now to certain proposals leading in this direction.

CHAPTER 6

Bridging the Chasm on Pennsylvania Avenue

"THE OTHER END OF THE AVENUE" IS A FAMILIAR PHRASE in Washington. A President is inaugurated at the Capitol.[1] He journeys along the historic mile of Pennsylvania Avenue, that famed thoroughfare which separates Capitol Hill from the White House. A colorful parade follows and tens of thousands cheer. Congress wishes the new Executive well, and there begins a political honeymoon of uncertain duration.

Almost invariably bickering arises, and one hears the phrase muttered in scorn or anger at both ends of the avenue. The statute mile of smooth paving between the physical habitats of the two branches of government lengthens into a seemingly unbridgeable chasm. The feuding becomes bitter and prolonged. Recall how Republican President Herbert Hoover was hamstrung after the Democrats captured the House in 1930. Government practically broke down while breadlines grew longer over the country. The division of governmental control and responsibility, at the time this book is being written, between a Republican Congress and a Democratic President, demonstrates the urgent necessity of workable machinery to effectuate cooperation.

---

[1] In 1945 the inauguration of Franklin Roosevelt for his fourth term was held on the White House portico—the only break in this tradition.

65

The need for closer collaboration between Congress and the administration frequently has been felt and voiced. So long as the United States was half empty, prosperous, and well protected by broad oceans, the old idea of balance of power maintained by dividing government into watertight compartments was tolerable. Now that the nation is crowded, harassed by weighty social and economic problems, and deeply involved in world affairs, better teamwork between the legislative and executive segments of government is essential to the welfare and security of the American people, and perhaps to the survival of the democratic system.

Many remedies have been suggested to cure this potentially dangerous gap in government. Some would scrap the check-and-balance system entirely and substitute the British parliamentary system. Others would make constitutional changes to create a hybrid of the two. The Constitution does make it easy for the executive and legislative branches to cherish their formal separation, if they are so disposed. It is equally certain that the Founding Fathers never intended the Republic should be without effective government. President Franklin D. Roosevelt summarized the situation when he said: "The letter of the Constitution wisely declared a separation, but the impulse of common purpose declares a union."

Nothing in the Constitution prevents practical procedures being devised to enable the two ends of Pennsylvania Avenue to work together in the formulation of legislation, instead of acting, too often, like antagonists in a struggle for power. Several such methods have been proposed. They range from a joint advisory group composed of Cabinet members and leaders of Congress meeting weekly, to mixed commissions like the Temporary National Economic Committee, on which sat representatives both of Congress and the administration.

Most of the disputes between the executive and legislative branches arise from a lack of facts on particular issues. An administrative head may get an excellent idea, or discover that a simple bill will solve a difficult problem. But sometimes he decides it is useless to try to get it through Congress, because he fears "those so-and-sos on the Hill never will study the facts."

More often a legislator gets fragmentary information from a constituent, reads a few paragraphs in a newspaper, or hears a part of a broadcast, then forthwith, and with all the comfortable immunity from libel that his remarks in the Senate or House enjoy, belabors some hapless official, or fires oral broadsides at an entire department. Occasionally this blind shooting hits a vulnerable target. At other times, Congress has been made to look petty, ridiculous, and deserving of the scorn of its bitterest critics. In a clear disregard of constitutional rights that any village lawyer would have recognized, the Congress in 1945 cut off the salaries of three officials, Robert Morss Lovett of the Interior Department, and Goodwin Watson and William E. Dodd, Jr., of the Foreign Broadcast Intelligence Division of the Federal Communications Commission, because they were suspected of holding views classed as "un-American." The Court of Claims promptly rebuked the legislative branch when the officials, who had had no trial and no chance to defend themselves, took their case to the bar for redress, and were sustained. Their salaries have since been paid.

Members constantly are tempted to fire with buckshot because no better ammunition is available. The endless succession of requests for investigations of this and that betray the fundamental lack of information that plagues senators and congressmen. In the 78th Congress there were two hundred seventeen requests made for specific information from the departments.

Congress needs data on the departments, on the administration of legislation to determine whether its intent is being followed, and, to an ever-increasing degree, Congress needs to be kept abreast of developments in foreign affairs. It all sums up to a crucial need for supplementing even a streamlined committee procedure: some way of giving members a better picture of the big overall issues confronting the nation, which would tend to make Congress more nationally and internationally minded.

The 1946 reorganization radically reduced the number of committees. However, before there was even time for the advantages of the new system to be demonstrated, both Senate and House were nullifying the 1946 gains by setting up several special committees. This fact makes it important to review the hardships visited upon administrators by any senseless multiplicity of committees. A few examples culled from the war Congresses illustrate the evil. When busy William Jeffers was working sixteen hours a day to solve the wartime rubber shortage, he was called before five committees during a single week. Paul McNutt and Donald Nelson, then heading the War Manpower Commission and the War Production Board, respectively, duplicated their statements before several House groups in one week. Mr. Nelson once said he thought that in one month he had appeared before *every* House committee.

Several committees had an interest in the problem of disposing of surplus property and war plants. The head of the War Assets Administration had this same time-wasting burden of repeat performances imposed on him as he gave his views to a succession of committees. Yet even under the simplified committee setup, the need remains for something more than a tiny percentage of the entire membership of Congress' getting a proper briefing on important issues. (The question of atomic energy transcends the jurisdiction of any single committee in either the Senate or House.)

This need was felt acutely by the Army during the war, and so a makeshift plan of addressing the Congress was devised. Secretary of War Henry Stimson, and then Under-Secretary Robert Patterson, with General George Marshall, the Chief of Staff, held informal meetings. Some of these sessions lasted three hours. When he succeeded General Marshall in the top Army job, General Dwight Eisenhower found Congress highly critical of demobilization and resorted to the same stratagem. A Baltimore *Sun* editorial dramatized the situation in some pointed, satiric observations:

"On Tuesday, General Eisenhower appeared before a large audience in the Library of Congress and made a speech. It was a good speech and on a gravely urgent subject. In a word, the general, as Chief of Staff, was telling Americans that if they want to keep conquered nations down, as all Americans do, they will have to have an army to do it with.

"What audience did the general choose to hear this speech? Oh, a Washington audience, mostly men in the middle or later years, bright men by their looks, fairly well off, intelligently interested in the subject matter. Any other thing to remark about the audience? Well, they did happen to be Members of Congress of the United States.

"But, if this was the Congress of the United States listening to a discussion of high state policy by the Chief of Staff on a question of supreme national import, why did it all take place in the Library of Congress? Why was the meeting procedurally and technically informal? Why were there no questions from the floor? Why was this historic confrontation of the military and the civilian legislative authority so carefully disguised as just such a public lecture as might have taken place at the grange hall in any rural village of the Republic? . . .

"But by and large, the fact that General Eisenhower, like Messrs. Stimson and Patterson before him, had to take this extraordinary and informal way of laying his case before the National Legislature argues a certain defect in our constitutional practice. . . ."

The *Sun's* satire is deserved. The executive branch of the government was running the show. Members of Congress were there to listen. There was no opportunity for questions or to direct the course of the discussion. It was after one of these lectures that the author decided to file a House resolution for a report and question period. Senator J. William Fulbright of Arkansas proposed a similar measure on his side of the Capitol. The *Sun* editorial went on to urge support of our proposal to remedy the situation it had so well described.

The objective is to provide an orderly and useful method of permitting Cabinet members and heads of federal agencies to meet Congress face to face on the floor of the Senate and House and talk things over. This report and question period, as the proposal is called, involves merely a change in the rules governing floor procedure in the Senate and House. No constitutional amendment is involved. The Constitution says (Article I, Section 5, Paragraph 2): "Each House may determine the rules of its proceedings. . . ."

The House resolution provided that no more than two hours shall be set aside, at least every two weeks but not more than once a week, to question administrative officials on the floor. The suggestions made previously in this volume show how this time can be found without upsetting the schedules of the two bodies.

During the first hour, the administrator would answer questions previously submitted in writing, approved by the committee having jurisdiction over his agency, and printed in the *Congressional Record*. The last hour, divided equally between the chairman and the ranking minority member of the committee issuing the invitation, would be given over to oral questions from the members of the whole House.

These questions would have to be germane to the preceding discussion. The Speaker would disallow and the administrator would not have to reply to an improper question. These are safeguards against heckling. Also, in time of war, some impromptu questions would have to be ruled out for reasons of national security. Under present organization, the Rules Committee would fix the length of time for each period, which in any case would not exceed two hours. It also would fix the priority of appearances in the event more than one invitation were pending at any one time. Under the simplified committee structure proposed here, this control would rest with the National Legislative Policy Committee.

The plan is as simple as that. No complicated parliamentary changes are necessary to put this constructive step into operation—only a simple amendment to the House rules. And the same holds true for the Senate.

The idea of a report and question period has been before the public long enough to appraise the nature of the opposition to it. Therefore, the authors wish to point out some things it is *not*, before outlining its positive advantages.

It does not infringe upon the spirit of the Constitution. It is not going to upset the balance of power between the divisions of the government. It does not contemplate substituting, now or in the future, the British or any other parliamentary system of government. It seeks neither to aggrandize nor impair the Executive's power. Congress would not be given any undue or unconstitutional authority over Cabinet members and agency heads. They are selected by the President and their service can be discontinued only by him. The legal relations between the President and Congress are altered in no way. And the report and question period is not conceived with any idea of partisan advantage to either the majority or the minority. But we do believe its operation will help shorten what often grows to be a long, long mile between the Capitol and the White House.

The plan seeks only to confer upon the executive heads a privilege and a duty to explain the operation of their respective departments and bureaus, present their problems, and furnish information that will enable Congress to legislate more intelligently and investigate with more light and less heat.

From the legislator's viewpoint, there would be a great gain in knowledge and background acquired in a manner far more economical of time and energy than any present available method, such as plodding through a thousand-page committee hearing. Committees, too, could lighten their work, if they had this means of informing the entire Congress of the organization and problems of departments they are supervising. It would provide a way of keeping all congressmen currently advised of the manner in which the executive agencies are administering the laws Congress passes. It would give administrators a chance to discuss their personnel, how they deal with the public, and to tell members of Congress what difficulties they encounter. The closest approach now to any member's getting this information is the specialized knowledge acquired by from five to nine persons sitting behind closed doors on an appropriations subcommittee and going over a departmental budget bill. And they only hear the hopes and woes of a single department or group of agencies.

One of the greatest results of a report and question period would be to establish the importance of Congress in the public mind. At present, executive heads hold news conferences. Radio and press reporters are assigned regularly to the more important departments. These news conferences are given more prominence in the newspapers and over the radio than action taken by Congress on important measures. If the plans and proposals for the administration of laws were brought out on the floors of the House and Senate pursuant to questions from members, the important news would arise from what was said on these occasions, rather than from what was said at some news conference "downtown."

Present methods may be satisfactory to the "oldsters" in Congress—those with twenty or thirty years of service. But we must consider the needs of the average member. Over the course of years, the votes cast in the House are by members who have an average tenure of slightly over two terms. The report and question period, handled in the spirit in which it is proposed, would be vastly useful in keeping all of Congress freshly informed as to the policies of the executive departments and the workings of their various bureaus. All these departments were established by Congress and spend billions of dollars which Congress authorizes. It is the duty of Congress to know what they are doing.

Advantages to the executive branch of the government are equally impressive. In making appointments, the President would have to keep in mind that his aides are going to be called upon to appear on the floors of the Senate and House. His administration would be judged, to a considerable extent, by the impressions these administrators made. It would be a compelling incentive to secure outstanding men for the key executive positions. The executive heads would gain an insight into the views of the people as expressed through the questions of their elected representatives. And these executive chiefs would consider more deliberately their decisions and administrative orders if they knew they might be called upon to render an official public accounting in the spotlight of an open House session.

There could be no ghost writing. These men would have to know their departments and be able to give the facts. The proposed system would be comparable to banking examinations. Banks keep their books in order all the time because they never know when the examiner will be around. Congress might not call a given agency chief before it for several years, but that agency chief never could be certain he was not on the immediate schedule, and would conduct his administration so as to be always prepared.

Unjust criticism often is made of executive officers or their practices. If it comes from a member of Congress, the executive involved generally has no opportunity to answer except through the radio and press. This further irritates the congressman who made the original charge. The report and question period would give the administrator an opportunity of explaining his side of a controversy where it could do the most good and where he still would be given adequate news coverage.

In the complex society of today it is necessary to concentrate much power in the Executive and allow wide discretion in the execution of general laws. This condition will continue and probably increase, regardless of the party in power. Appearances before Congress would require Cabinet members and administrative chiefs to formulate clear definitions of executive policies. Sometimes these officials do not know what the President's policy is on certain matters under their jurisdiction. This is no reflection on the present executive establishment. The same condition has always existed. Before an executive head appeared at a question period, he naturally would call upon the President to define clearly the policy in regard to matters on which the official was to be questioned.

At a lower level, the executive chief himself would have to make up his mind on many questions he may dodge now.

Faced with an invitation to make a personal report to Congress, he would be taking a great risk if he did not settle those undetermined factors affecting his department before submitting to interrogation. Would it not have been a great help if then Secretary of State James F. Byrnes had appeared on occasion before the entire Senate and House to give information about the workings of United States foreign policy, and more particularly about the Russian impasse? The same would have held true for Wilson Wyatt after he had formulated and was executing his program to deal with the housing crisis. Much fog would have been dispelled if the Secretary of the Treasury could have appeared at a report period to give his opinion and answer questions regarding the twenty per cent "across the board" reduction of income taxes proposed by Republican leadership.

The report and question period may sound very precedent shattering, unorthodox—even radical. Actually it is as old as Congress itself. Many of the men who framed the Constitution were also members of the First Congress. When the law organizing the Treasury Department was passed in 1789, it was made the duty of the Secretary of the Treasury to "make reports and give information to either branch of the legislature, in person or in writing, as he may be required, respecting all matters which may be referred to him by the Senate or House of Representatives or which shall appertain to his office."

Objection was made in debate that this might lead to having all the Cabinet secretaries on the floor. Nevertheless, the bill passed. The record also shows that on July 22, 1789, "The Secretary of Foreign Affairs attended, agreeably to order, and made the necessary explanations." The next month, the *Annals of Congress* reports that "The President of the United States came into the Senate Chamber attended by

General Knox, Secretary of War, and laid before the Senate the following statement of facts with the questions hereto annexed, for their advice and consent."

Historians say that Washington did not like the treatment he received before the Senate, because when asked to appear he was kept waiting for two days. However, the appearance of his Cabinet members and the message sent up in 1790 advising the Senate that the Secretary of War would "attend them" to discuss an Indian tribe treaty, shows that the Father of His Country, who had presided over the Constitutional Convention, used and thought well of the personal report system in his administration. There are about fourteen references to a member of the executive branch's appearing before the Senate during the First Congress. The *Congressional Globe* cites eight similar instances in the House. Unfortunately, the records are not clear as to what took place and it is fair to say that probably the Cabinet member acted largely as a courier.

President Jefferson discontinued the practice of addressing Congress in person. When Woodrow Wilson revived it more than a century later, there was considerable criticism on the theory that such appearances were not in keeping with tradition. The record is against the critics. It was a policy open to the President under the Constitution. In the same manner, the proposal advanced here is open to the United States today because of the wisdom of the men who wrote its basic law.

Historical interest is found in the fact that the men who wrote the constitution of the Confederate States did include a specific provision authorizing appearance of cabinet members in the legislative forum. The chairman of the convention who drafted that document was Alexander Stephens of Georgia, one of the great statesmen of his time. He held that the lack of consultation and coordination between the legislative branches and the Executive was one of the weaknesses of the Federal Government which the new government for the seceding states should avoid. Under his leadership, the provisions prohibiting a member of the legislative branch from holding office in the executive establishment were incorporated, but with this important sentence which is not in the United States Constitution: "But congress may, by law, grant to the principal officer in each of the executive departments a seat upon the floor of either house, with the privilege of discussing any measures appertaining to his department." Unfortunately, the necessary legislation to implement this language was not enacted under the Jefferson Davis administration of the Confederacy.

A bill to permit heads of executive departments to occupy seats on the floor of the House was reported unanimously in 1864 by a select committee headed by Representative George H. Pendleton of Ohio. The war emergency caused it to be shunted aside but Pendleton revived it in 1881 when he was a senator. He headed another committee which included Senator James G. Blaine, twice Secretary of State and later a Republican presidential candidate, Senator W. B. Allison, who served thirty-five years in the upper chamber, and other distinguished members. Again there was a unanimous report for adoption. The movement failed apparently because it made attendance of the administrators compulsory, and some felt this would interfere with the work of Congress. Others said Congress would be exalted over the Executive, and vice versa. Committees were apprehensive that they would be supplanted. The report and question period as described here avoids all of these objections.

The Pendleton resolution failed in the House because a member made a dramatic speech about "aping England." Feeling against Britain at that time was running high because of her open aid to the Confederacy, and the argument was effective. Actually, the device is truly American, planned to operate entirely within the present American constitutional framework. However, if it can remotely be called an English idea, one does well to remember that English common law, the bill of rights, and habeas corpus also were great British traditions which the United States adopted and which have meant much to the American people.

There is abundant contemporary support for the plan. President William Howard Taft, in his annual message in 1912, said: ". . . I do not think that I am mistaken in saying that the presence of members of the Cabinet on the floor of each House would greatly contribute to the enactment of legislation." Similar views have been advanced in their time by Chief Justice Charles Evans Hughes, Elihu Root, John W. Davis, President James A. Garfield, President Woodrow Wilson, President Herbert Hoover, Dr. Nicholas Murray Butler, Dr. Charles A. Beard, Walter P. Armstrong, and a host of others.

We have consulted many thoughtful members of both parties who endorse the proposal. It has wide popular support. A Gallup poll showed that seven out of every ten persons interviewed favored the report and question plan. Only seven out of every hundred were against it. More than three hundred newspapers and publications, Democratic, Republican, and Independent, including such esteemed journals as the New York *Times,* the St. Louis *Post-Dispatch,* The Baltimore *Sun,* the Washington *Post,* the Raleigh *News and Observer,* the Nashville *Tennessean,* and the Washington *Star* have urged its adoption in some form in numerous articles and editorials.

Americans are entering the most important and challenging period of their own and of world history. The form of government that has endured such great crises as the War Between The States may be facing even more crucial tests. No problem on the present agenda of democracy has a higher priority than that of inducing closer, stronger, steadier cooperation between the President and the Congress. We believe that the report and question proposal is a healthy step in this direction.

CHAPTER 7

Closing a Gap in Democracy

THE NEW AND DANGEROUS AGGRESSION OF THE SOVIET UNION might have been bridled at San Francisco in the spring of 1945 had not the great moral power of the United States been handcuffed to history by the dangerous and undemocratic provision of the Constitution requiring a two-thirds concurrence of the Senate to ratify a treaty.

It was the final hour for Nazi Germany. The Soviet Union was impressed with American military power, then at its zenith in Europe. The nations of the world had gathered at the United Nations Organization meeting to hammer out a charter to ensure world peace. The crucial issue emerged quickly. The Russians insisted on world domination by the great powers through the proposed Security Council, and on the right of any one of the "Big Five" to paralyze even the Council by the exercise of an all-inclusive veto. The small- and medium-sized nations instantly recognized this veto as dooming their hopes for practical protection against the aggression of a strong and willful neighbor.

The great American democracy had long been the champion of the rights of the "little peoples" of the world. The latter turned their eyes to the United States as they had done in 1919. Had not a great wartime Secretary of State, Cordell

Hull, firmly embedded in the already illustrious foreign policy of the United States the principle of extending aid to any nation threatened by unwarranted aggression? An overwhelming majority of the American people had indicated by every conceivable register of public will, including a national election, that it supported the formation of a strong world organization based upon democratic principles.

It is our conviction that if the United States delegation had attacked the Russian proposals boldly, Moscow would have compromised rather than risk the entire blame for failure of the first attempt to blueprint a lasting peace. However, the Russians as well as the American representatives knew there remained in the Senate a small hard core of isolationists and extreme nationalists. The Russians knew the United States Constitution just as well as did this country's own representatives at San Francisco. The two-thirds rule was not discussed very often in the daily deliberations of the Americans, but no American delegate forgot for a moment that any charter adopted at San Francisco could be killed by one-third plus one of the membership of the Senate. This ancient rule stood in the background like a guillotine, its blade still encrusted with the blood of the Treaty of Versailles and the League of Nations which it had decapitated a quarter-century before. The Russians knew as well as the Americans that the veto provision was the same kind of rock as that on which the "little band of irreconcilables" took their successful stand in the Senate in 1919 to defeat Woodrow Wilson and the League. So the world saw the United States range itself on the side of strong-arm tactics, persuade a wavering Britain to go along, and let doughty little Australia make the unequal fight for a more liberal world organization.

This single illustration shows how vitally the future of this country is tied to the reorganization of congressional procedures. It fortifies our belief that in its long-range implications for Congress and the people, one of the most important recommendations in this book is that by constitutional amendment the two-thirds provision be abolished. The House should be permitted to participate on an equal basis with the Senate in determining the future international relations of the United States by making treaties subject to ratification by a majority vote of both houses, as is the case with all other legislation.

The two-thirds rule originated in a political compromise; its application places dictatorial powers in the hands of a few; it has resulted, especially in recent years, in the use of subterfuges that menace the functions of the legislative branch; its retention prevents the full force of this nation from being exerted in the world, and its abolition would remove from the Constitution one of the great remaining barriers to the development of full democracy in the two branches of Congress.

The Constitution says in Article II, Section 2, that "He [the President] shall have power, by and with the advice and consent of the Senate, to make treaties, provided two thirds of the Senators present concur. . . ." Thus it could happen that the fate of the nation might some day lie in the hands of just thirty-three senators representing only eight per cent of the people. This assumes that all ninety-six members are voting. At the other possible, although unlikely, extreme, if only a quorum (49) was on hand, seventeen senators from nine states having only three per cent of the population might kill a treaty that had almost universal support. (Comparisons are based on the seventeen least populous states as shown in the 1940 census.)

No fundamental philosophy of government was involved in the origin of this curious anachronism. Discussion in the Constitutional Convention of the application of treaties to the future welfare of the nation as a whole did not figure in deciding what procedure would make these documents part of the supreme law of the land. Insertion of the two-thirds rule was an expedient used to mollify the suspicions, differences, and jealousies of the thirteen original states.

Its adoption was the culmination of a long and heated struggle which had been going on since the signing of the Declaration of Independence, which found expression in the Articles of Confederation, and which, in fact, almost prevented the union of the states.

The Northern and Southern states were seeking to preserve what each group regarded as its special interests. The four Southern states wanted to protect navigation on the Mississippi, and the future of New Orleans as a port. The four New England states were interested in safeguarding their fishery rights. If either group of four could get the vote of one other state, it would be able to block any treaty affecting the local interests of that group. The dispute between the sections became so dangerous and violent that James Monroe of Virginia proposed that the United States be divided into three nations: a southern, a middle, and a northern confederacy. Friends, however, dissuaded him from pressing this proposal. These differences, and the fear of the smaller states that the larger ones might unduly dominate them, were the underlying causes for the inclusion of the two-thirds rule in the Constitution.

The clause is a striking example of a provision inserted to take care of a burning political issue of the times. It was a compromise to unite thirteen states into a union. The union has long since been created and firmly cemented. We must study the effect of this provision in dealing with foreign affairs in an advanced era never visualized by the architects of the Constitution.

The Founding Fathers held no firm convictions that

treaties with foreign nations should be ratified by two-thirds of the Senate. In fact, on September 7, 1787, a motion to exclude "treaties of peace" from the two-thirds provision was adopted without dissent by the Constitutional Convention. The following day the action was reversed. However, there were at least three definite reasons for denying the House the right to participate in treaty-making.

It was contemplated that the President would actually advise and consult with the senators, who numbered twenty-six when the Constitution was adopted, and that the Senate would be an expert body which would work with him in the formulation of treaties. Accordingly, in the initial session of Congress, President Washington tried personally to advise and consult with the Senate concerning a treaty with the Creek Indians. We have noted previously what happened. The First President did not again expose himself to such cool treatment. Since that time, treaties have been handled by the Senate as other legislation. The "advice" provision of the treaty clause became obsolete. The Senate never entered into the active negotiation of treaties, as was envisioned by the founders, until Secretary Hull's regime.

It also was anticipated that treaties would be made in executive or secret sessions of a small Senate, with the President attending. Secrecy no longer plays a part in treaty ratifications. The present Senate has more members (96) than the House had at the time of the First Congress (66).

Finally, under the Constitution as originally written, senators being elected by the state legislatures, it was thought that they would have greatly superior knowledge of foreign affairs as compared with the House members, and that their longer terms of service would give them a broader grasp of treaty problems. Since 1913, senators have been elected directly by the people in exactly the same fashion as representatives, and the first of these reasons has ceased to be valid.

Furthermore, history demonstrates that the tenure argument is no longer logical or sustainable.

Hamilton, in *The Federalist,* expressed the prevailing idea that "the fluctuating and multitudinous composition" of the House would unfit it for a share in treaty-making. Of course, Hamilton could not foresee that the negotiation of treaties would be taken over by the Executive, leaving to the Senate only the duty of passing judgment on documents already signed.

The record of the Senate in handling treaties of peace with the two-thirds rule is long, and it is disturbingly bad. From the moment the United States became a world power as a result of the Spanish-American War, up to the United Nations Charter, the Senate has frustrated every significant move to make it possible for the country to participate in settling international disputes. It rejected the Olney-Pauncefote arbitration treaty of 1897. It emasculated the Hay arbitration treaties of 1904, an act which led John Hay, President McKinley's able Secretary of State, to observe that "a treaty entering the Senate is like a bull going into the arena; no one can say just when or how the final blow will fall— but one thing is certain, it will never leave the arena alive." The Senate next retained a stranglehold on the innocuous Root arbitration treaties of 1908-10, and impeded the efforts of President Taft to advance the Taft arbitration treaties of 1911.

The history of what happened to the Treaty of Versailles, the League of Nations, and the World Court following World War I is well known to all. It is dramatically emphasized in the great motion picture *Wilson,* which most readers doubtless have seen. At one point, Wilson is shown arguing with the "Tiger of France," Georges Clemenceau, over the latter's demand for the Saar Basin and the Rhineland. The World War I President insisted that the French live up to the terms of the Armistice regarding the right of self-determination, and write a treaty conforming to the spirit of the proposed League of Nations. Whereupon, in the film, Clemenceau asks Wilson: "Are you aware that a bloc of thirty-seven senators have signed a resolution stating that the League, as you propose it, is not acceptable to the American people?" Clemenceau knew the Constitution too.

The scenario writer took liberties with the lines, but the facts of what happened at Paris and afterward led Stuart Perry, prominent journalist of that day, to write: "The course of the Senate in disposing of the Four Power treaty confirms the conclusion drawn from its treatment of the Versailles Treaty, that the requirement of a two-thirds vote combined with the normal operation of party politics has impaired the treaty-making power of this country to a dangerous degree." A high-ranking State Department official, speaking privately, said the effect of the provision was to send American representatives into the diplomatic arena with one hand tied behind their backs.

The State Department, acting under direction of the President, may desire to carry out a foreign policy it believes accords with the interests of the American people, but often it is required to follow a course it may feel morally wrong and constitutionally undesirable. It must water down its execution so as not to risk defeat of the administration at the hands of a small Senate minority.

No administration can feel sure of its grounds in concluding treaties. We cited at the beginning of this chapter an example of how we believe United States prestige is impaired and United States leadership weakened at world conferences. The peoples of other nations know that Americans have magnificent impulses but cannot make them effective. In 1918, as in 1945, they saw this country stand on a high level of world leadership never before attained by any people. After 1918, they watched the United States become gripped by fratricidal political war for two whole years. They saw her held helpless in the vise of the treaty veto until she had been confused, embittered, and removed from world affairs as a constructive force. For twenty years she was to drift, a mighty and dangerous derelict on an ocean of world anarchy. Now they have seen her in 1945 make a "practical" compromise to avoid a duplication of this malodorous chapter in her history.

At the moment, the United States is making a brilliant effort to overcome the limitations of the Charter. She is taking a leading role in the United Nations councils, and is accepting her responsibility for full-fledged participation in international affairs. But the approval of the Charter by the Senate with only two dissenting votes does not alter the necessity of modifying the outworn two-thirds rule.

There might have been no such auspicious beginning if issues such as Lend-Lease, the United Nations Relief and Rehabilitation Administration, and the British loan had been sent to the Capitol in the form of treaties. Under the two-thirds rule, none of these three measures would have passed the Senate. In the years to come, treaties in which this nation will be called upon to participate will be presented in increasing numbers. Treaties growing out of the Charter will be more controversial than the Charter itself.

When the international relations of the United States were few and simple, when the oceans really protected her, the emasculation and rejection of treaties by a minority of the Senate could be tolerated. Today modern science and invention have made the frontiers of all nations almost contiguous. Today, as the greatest democratic nation in the world, the responsibility for leadership in achieving world peace is thrust upon her. Two world wars in one generation demonstrate that she cannot shrink from this place of leadership and survive as a free nation. Events in any part of the world directly or indirectly affect her economy and welfare. If the United States is to survive, she must be able to function effectively in foreign affairs.

Royal monarchs and dictatorships are undeniably efficient in foreign relations. King Ibn Saud speaks with unquestioned authority for Saudi Arabia. Premier Joseph Stalin calls the turn for the Soviet Union. Whoever is Prime Minister of Britain usually can act with great authority, as his decisions need to be sustained only by a majority of the British House of Commons. When the very life or death of this nation may depend on fast-working, efficient machinery for handling international relations, the problem is to preserve the right of the people, through Congress, to participate in the grave issues. The present system by which 34 out of 531 chosen representatives of the people in Congress can block the fulfilment of the will of a majority of the people, damages the treaty-making power of this great nation, and can hamstring efforts of the President and his Secretary of State to devise and execute effective foreign policy.

It is not surprising, therefore, that Congress and the nation have acquiesced in frequent resort to dodges and evasions to overcome this constitutional handicap. *A most important point,* which is not generally realized, is that such subterfuge, absolutely necessary for government to function effectively, is robbing Congress of legislative powers that it should exercise more fully today than ever before in its history.

This circumvention of the Constitution usually takes the form of an executive agreement whereby the President, together with the Secretary of State or even a lesser official, commits the nation formally, through a signed instrument, to a course of action that in many cases should have been the subject of a treaty. Congress often joins in this evasion by supporting the executive branch with a concurrent resolution—a legislative formality that normally does not have the force of law but merely expresses the feeling of Congress on a particular subject. Treaties, under the Constitution, become part of the supreme law of the land. These subterfuges do not. When they are employed, American prestige and integrity in the field of international law suffer accordingly.

Presidents of the United States, particularly during the past fifty years, have been forced to use these devices to accomplish the desire of the people because of the well-founded fear of not being able to get two-thirds of the Senate to approve a particular issue. Thus does the operation of an outmoded rule tend to place the foreign affairs of the nation more and more in the hands of the executive branch, to the practical exclusion of Congress.

The two-thirds provision prevented the annexation of the Republic of Texas (1845) and the Hawaiian Islands (1898) to the United States by treaty. The Bretton Woods agreement, UNRRA, and the International Labor Agreement are examples of recent commitments which should have been drafted and submitted as treaties rather than as agreements.

A tabulation reveals that, up to 1939, the United States signed almost 2000 international instruments. Of this number, 1182 were executive agreements; 799 were treaties. We do not condemn the agreements as illegal. Most of them were necessary for the welfare of the country and have subsequently been approved by Congress, but many should have been submitted as treaties.

The tendency is unhealthy. The two-thirds rule, instead of working to maintain great power in the Senate, actually is taking away that power. Under strong Presidents, with wide public support, it could lead to the virtual elimination of Congress from the vital field of foreign affairs, where the wisdom and experience of the people's representatives should be used as a check upon the powers and decisions of the Executive.

Two important by-products would result from adoption of the proposed constitutional amendment. First, there would be removed a cancerous source of estrangement between Congress and the Executive. The amendment would unquestionably promote a more effective relationship between the two ends of Pennsylvania Avenue. Neither the Senate nor the House looks with particular favor on the growing practice of settling problems of treaty level by executive agreements. Yet the Executive is tempted continuously to use the method because of fear of the Senate minority.

The second by-product would be elimination of the greatest single cause of antagonism between the two houses of the national legislature. Bad blood has frequently come out in the open. The House always has insisted that when legislative stipulations are inserted in a treaty, "it is the constitutional right and duty of the House of Representatives, in all such cases, to deliberate on the expediency or inexpediency of carrying such treaty into effect." Language to that effect was in a resolution adopted by the House in 1871 without debate; the opinion remains as the settled attitude of the lower chamber.

Support for this position goes as far back as Thomas Jefferson's day. He wrote Madison in March, 1796, saying that he thought the House, as one branch of the legislature, was perfectly free to refuse its assent, when a treaty included matters confided by the Constitution to the whole legislature, in all cases "when in its judgment the good of the people would not be served by letting the treaty go into effect."

When the Jay treaty controversy was inflaming the country, the Virginia legislature adopted a resolution recommending adoption of a constitutional amendment providing that no treaty containing any stipulation upon the subject of the powers vested in Congress should become the supreme law of the land until it should have been approved in those particulars by a majority in the House of Representatives, and that the President, before he ratified any treaty, should submit the same to the House of Representatives.

In 1868 the House took a decided stand against including legislation within a treaty without the previous assent of Congress. The Alaska treaty not only stipulated that the United States should pay $7,200,000 to the Emperor of Russia, but that certain inhabitants of Alaska should be admitted to the privileges and immunities of citizens of the United States. The House was angry. It retaliated with its own constitutional prerogative to initiate or withhold appropriations. The bill providing the purchase money declared that the stipulations of the Alaska treaty could not be carried into full force and effect except by legislation agreed to by both houses of Congress. Then, by a 98 to 49 vote, the House reaffirmed its right to pass on these stipulations and did approve them.

In the 79th Congress, the House passed, by the necessary two-thirds vote, a resolution proposing the submission to the states of a constitutional amendment empowering both houses of Congress to participate in approving treaties. This House-approved measure gathered dust in the files of the Senate Judiciary Committee. The refusal of the Senate even to consider the proposal hardly serves to decrease the antagonism between the two bodies.

So far, we have presented a somewhat negative outline of the dangers and bad effects of the two-thirds rule. It would be a method of terminating the subterfuges and the power of a stubborn Senate minority to ask merely that the rule be altered to require only a majority in the Senate for approval of treaties. But the change must be more basic than that, and so we come now to consider the good and affirmative reasons why the House should share equally with the other chamber in shaping foreign policy.

We have disposed of the reasons given by the Founding Fathers, which rested on the assumed superior capabilities of senators over representatives and on the necessity for secrecy. What happened in this country in 1944-45, from Dumbarton Oaks to the ratification of the United Nations Charter, simply was beyond the imagination of the eighteenth-century leaders. The complex subject of methods of world cooperation was debated and discussed in cities and crossroads in every state in the union, over a thousand radio stations and in uncounted millions of words printed in more than one hundred thousand publications ranging from great dailies and weekly magazines to mimeographed bulletins of tiny community organizations. Practically all the people participated and are participating in some measure in their country's foreign relations.

Members of the House are traditionally closer to the people and in a better position to exert leadership and act in accordance with the desire of the majority. No foreign policy agreed upon by the Senate can long endure unless it has the support of the people. If that policy has the sanction of a majority of both Senate and House, it is undeniably the foreign policy of the nation. Having this sanction, it will receive better and more enlightened support from the people.

Under the proposed system, there normally would be a lapse of time between action by the two houses, just as there is on other legislation. This would give public opinion an opportunity to operate after it had the facts brought out in the initial debate in whatever chamber first considered the treaty. And this opportunity for a reappraisal of important issues is one of the basic reasons for a bicameral legislative system.

Today and in the future, much of the nation's important domestic legislation is necessarily closely interwoven with its foreign policy. Laws affecting the Merchant Marine, size of the Army and Navy, the merger of the armed services, giving or exchanging materials of war, regulation of radio and aviation, tariffs and long-range agricultural policies, all pertain directly to foreign affairs, and all such legislation requires the concurrence of both houses of Congress.

In many of these areas, to use agriculture and aviation as examples, the treaties and agreements involving other nations will grow greatly in number and importance. Few treaties are self-executing or can long be sustained without implementing legislation, which *both* houses must pass. Appropriations and legislation usually are imperative to give full effect to any international agreement to which the United States adheres. We see no valid reason why an exception should be made in the case of treaties, when by one device or another they must secure the approval of the House.

Under the Constitution, as has been noted, treaties are declared to be a part of the supreme law of the land, along with the Constitution itself and laws passed in pursuance thereof. This legislative status is an important reason for associating both congressional bodies in the treaty-making process. It is an important reason for permitting them to act by the same majority which suffices for other legislation. At present it is possible for a bare majority in Congress to abrogate a treaty by passing conflicting legislation, or by failing to pass subsidiary legislation necessary to carry out its provisions. Such action leaves the treaty in existence as an international obligation, but as the law of the land the treaty is overruled and of no effect. This creates poor relationships with other countries.

The final positive reason for the proposed alteration in the treaty-making process is the one expressed in the title to this chapter—to close a gap in democracy. We recognize that inexperience in setting up a government that would "derive its just powers from the consent of the governed," plus actual fear of "the mob," caused the provisions to be inserted in the Constitution that make popular government difficult today. Most of the history of amendments to that document is a study of the successful efforts of the people to undo the original checks and balances designed to hamstring their will.

The people were originally denied the right to elect their President and Vice-President. By 1804, the choosing of the electors had been placed in the hands of the voters, although there are many who think this particular mechanism is due for another change. Next came the Reconstruction amendments abolishing slavery and affirming the right of all Americans to citizenship and suffrage. In 1913, the anachronism of the people's not being trusted to elect members of the Senate was removed from the Constitution, and the right to levy taxes on those most able to pay for the support of the government was added.

Nationwide suffrage was extended in 1920 to women through the adoption of the Nineteenth Amendment. Thirteen years later the people followed the great leadership of George Norris and, in the Twentieth Amendment, abolished the "lame duck" sessions of Congress, thus bringing the supreme legislative body even closer to those it represents. There still remains this two-thirds rule in Article II of the Constitution. It is one of the most undemocratic provisions left in the national charter.

The League of Women Voters made the reorganization

of Congress and the amending of the two-thirds rule its number-one domestic legislative project for 1946-47. The League properly combined the two proposals. Indeed, no plan to strengthen Congress can be complete without including the change of this rule. Experience with the two-thirds provision has been very costly. The price may be even greater if it is retained.

CHAPTER 8

Making Party Responsibility Mean Something

"THE GENTLEMEN ON THE OTHER SIDE OF THE AISLE" IS AN
expression heard frequently in partisan debate in the Senate
and House. It refers, of course, to the seating in the respective chambers of the majority and minority party members
on opposite sides of the room.

The phrase also symbolizes the fact that America's is a government by two great political organizations, the Democratic
and Republican parties. Any study of congressional reorganization would be incomplete if it did not consider the effect
of party machinery, or the lack thereof, on the efficient
functioning of the national legislature.

There were no party labels attached to the gifted band of
leaders who staked out the American form of government
in the constitutional debates of more than a century and a
half ago. These political pioneers did not envision political
parties as they exist today.

They anticipated that candidates for Congress would assert
their own platforms without coming under party designa-
tions, and that once elected, each would be entirely free to
carry out his own will. It soon developed, however, to the
dismay of President George Washington, that members could
be more effective by joining with others having similar views

and objectives. Also, early experience showed the necessity of forming organizations to enable the orderly presentation of the pros and cons of public questions.

Since 1800, the government has been controlled by parties. With few exceptions, the two-party system has prevailed. There have been historic rebellions within the major parties. The most spectacular in recent history occurred in 1912 when ex-President Theodore Roosevelt and his "Bull Moosers" bolted the Republican organization and won a Pyrrhic victory over President William Howard Taft seeking reelection. The split gave the election to the Democrats and Woodrow Wilson.

Another schism occurred in 1924 when Senator Robert M. La Follette, Sr., a Republican, organized the Progressive party with Senator Burton K. Wheeler of Montana, a Democrat, as his running mate. The ticket carried only La Follette's home state of Wisconsin. Minor parties come and go. In the last three national elections, the Socialist, Prohibition, and Communist parties have put up candidates, but they have attracted only minor fractions of the total vote.

A two-party system is the most logical, responsive, and successful method yet devised for operating a republican form of government. One party has the responsibility of formulating and carrying out a legislative program. The minority party is the "opposition." This does not mean it opposes every move of the majority. There are always large areas of agreement. This is especially true in the field of foreign affairs. The minority should put forth a better program if it can; it should suggest and try to force improvements in the majority's plan, and at all times it should be constructively critical. Every party is supposed to have a set of basic concepts or principles upon which it stands. Its duty is to fight vigorously for those principles and try to get the majority of voters to accept them and thereby give it the control of the government.

Democracies having more than two parties always have had confusion, bordering at times on chaos, in their representative legislative bodies. No party can win a majority, and the result is unstable and unhealthy coalitions. Prewar France is a good example. With five or six parties, no one group had definite responsibility and the issues up for decision by the people were never clearcut. This accounted for the frequent changes in the control of the French Government. Even today, in France's crucial struggle for recovery, the plague of multiple parties remains. The small Liberal party in the British House of Commons in recent years has attached itself to the Labor party, and as a separate group has largely lost its usefulness.

Unfortunately, in this country labels have come to mean little. There is not now a well-defined difference in the political and economic philosophy of the Democratic and Republican parties. Some politicians say one is "liberal" and the other "conservative." Here one runs into trouble with the meaning of those terms. But taking the usual definition, one finds many "conservatives" in the Democratic fold and many "liberals" in Republican ranks. The two parties should be differentiated clearly from each other. The state of the union would be healthier if their platforms and programs were more clearly defined. Thus the voter would be able to decide more intelligently which party he wanted in control. Comparing the 1944 platforms of the Democrats and the GOP, one finds very few fundamental deviations.

As matters stand, the organizations are loosely formed. Few substantial differences are presented for decision. Each party endeavors to capture groups and classes of voters by an elastic manipulation of its platform. This happens every four years. In the interim, there is little organizational or educational work done by either party. One prominent Republican, former Governor Harold Stassen of Minnesota, through his political forums is making some headway in trying to crystallize political thought. This type of political education should be expanded broadly by both parties. Without reference to the merits of its policies, the Political Action Committee formed by the Congress of Industrial Organizations, utilizing long-established political techniques, showed the two parties a lesson in organization. The PAC had a program, kept its followers informed about its objectives, and, in sections where it had members, put on a systematic ward and precinct campaign. It is alarming that this is not done more by the major parties themselves. It is a basic type of political activity that cannot be left to a group representing a distinct class interest, if the two-party system is to survive in its most useful form.

We turn now to the party machinery on Capitol Hill. Naturally, the health and efficiency of the major parties affect the conduct of business by the national legislature. The most important political mechanism is the caucus or conference. This is a private meeting of members of a political party to select candidates to fill the various official posts in the Senate and House, to nominate members to serve on the committees, to discuss legislation with a view to concerted action, to lay down the "party line" on particular issues.

The Democrats call these party meetings caucuses while the Republicans usually term their gatherings conferences. We shall refer hereinafter particularly to the workings of the Democratic party since we are more familiar with its operation, and its shortcomings have been more conspicuous.

If a visitor to the Senate and House Office Buildings opens

the imposing doors marked "Caucus Room," he will behold the largest and finest assembly halls on Capitol Hill, excepting the actual meeting chambers of the two houses. However, for more than a decade, these huge rooms have been used principally to hold committee hearings that drew crowds too large for the regular committee quarters. They have also housed exhibits, and have been utilized to give members of Congress previews of important documentary or historical films.

When these buildings were planned in 1905, it was a different story. The caucus was then a device used frequently by both parties, which accounts for the importance given to the caucus rooms in the blueprints. An interesting story is told of Champ Clark. In 1909 he was chosen Minority Leader of the House Democrats, succeeding John Sharp Williams of Mississippi who had been elected to the Senate. The Democratic minority had been going in a dozen directions at once and there had been little party control. Champ Clark came home about three o'clock one morning in 1909. He explained to Mrs. Clark he was very tired because the Democrats had been having a caucus for seven hours. But he said the party had been reorganized and it would now work with real discipline in the House. Mrs. Clark asked, "How did you do it?" Champ Clark's reply was, "We let everybody talk himself out." The Democrats adopted a program, furnished leadership, and carried the House in 1911. Champ Clark was elected Speaker.

A glance at two important rules governing Democratic caucuses indicates the extent of party discipline that may be expected if this mechanism is used effectively. The author had considerable difficulty in locating a copy of these rules which still, theoretically, are in effect.

Rules 7 and 8 provide:

"7. In deciding upon action in the House involving party policy or principle, a two-thirds vote of those present and voting at a Caucus meeting shall bind all members of the Caucus: Provided, The said two-thirds vote is a majority of the full Democratic membership of the House; And provided further, That no member shall be bound upon questions involving a construction of the Constitution of the United States or upon which he made contrary pledges to his constituents prior to his election or received contrary instructions by resolutions or platform from his nominating authority.

"8. Whenever any member of the Caucus shall determine, by reason of either of the exceptions provided for in the above paragraph, not to be bound by the action of the Caucus on those questions, it shall be his duty, if present, so to advise the Caucus before the adjournment of the meeting, or if not present at the meeting, to promptly notify the Democratic leader in writing, so that the party may be advised before the matter comes to issue upon the Floor of the House."

For years after Champ Clark was made party leader in 1909 the House Democrats had frequent caucuses. They were lengthy and vigorous sessions. Party differences were settled there. If the party was bound to some policy by a two-thirds vote under Rule 7, a few members usually arose and asked to "recuse" themselves, giving one of the reasons set out in Rule 7—a contrary pledge to constituents, or disagreement on the question of constitutionality. "Recuse" is a word found only in the dictionary today, but it was well known to Democratic caucuses of years past.

During President Wilson's administration the caucus operated with telling effectiveness. The success that Wilson had during his first term in getting congressional approval of the major part of his legislative program, including passage of the Federal Reserve Act, always has been considered one of his greatest achievements. Much credit is due Wilson's vision and leadership, but equal credit is due to the effective way the Democratic party made use of its caucuses in both houses of Congress. During this time the party adopted the policy of considering every major measure in caucus, and of binding the members to abide by the decision of that caucus. The Speaker and the Majority Leader then knew exactly where they stood. They knew whether they could put a bill through without amendment or whether it would be necessary to make compromises to win votes from the minority.

Traditionally, party control is better among the Republicans than the Democrats. With the exceptions already noted, the GOP has operated smoothly and efficiently in the long periods since 1861 when it has been the majority party in one or both houses. A succession of strong Republican Speakers in the House held the party reins tightly. In the Senate, an occasional flurry of a few independent freshmen, dubbed, in one instance, the "Young Turks," has not marred the general responsiveness of Republican senators to the policies laid down in GOP conferences.

In the 79th, and for several preceding Congresses, Representative Roy O. Woodruff of Michigan was chairman of the Republican conference. He worked in close cooperation with the then Minority Leader Joseph W. Martin, Jr., of Massachusetts. Congressman Woodruff called a conference of Republican House members to consider most of the principal issues; he advised us that eight conferences were held during the 79th Congress. They lasted from one to four hours. Every member was encouraged to express himself and could talk as long as he wished. The Republicans made no effort to bind the conference, but usually when the meeting was over the membership was almost unanimous in its position. The secret, said Representative Woodruff, was to "let everyone have his say and get his peeves off his chest." Similarly, in the Senate, the Republican members met frequently to discuss party reaction and policy on major issues.

The Democrats, on the other hand, just quit having caucuses on issues. They still had sessions at the opening of a Congress to nominate House officers and rubber-stamp recommendations for committee appointments. But in the House, where for sixteen years they had the responsibility of leadership, the Democrats did not use the valuable technique of the caucus, and this accounts in part for their failure to retain control in the 1946 congressional election. We assume leaders of the party considered these meetings too risky. One, held at the beginning of the special session of 1933, very nearly committed the party against the Economy Act which President Roosevelt had recommended. Later, in 1938, when a caucus was called to consider the Fair Labor Standards Act, a quorum could not be secured and the caucus was never held. This was the last effort. No caucuses were held on Lend-Lease, Selective Service, Arms Embargo, Full Employment, Housing, OPA, or any of the major bills which were presented to the House during recent years.

During the 79th Congress, the House journal shows the Democrats had only one other caucus after the opening meeting. It was called upon petition of fifty members to adopt a resolution criticizing the chairman of the Democratic National Comittee, Robert Hannegan, for a letter his office had written. And this was not calculated to further party harmony.

The results of this situation were obvious. During the 79th Congress, it frequently happened that enough Democratic members voted with the Republicans so as to give the Republicans virtual control of particular legislation.

But on both sides of the aisle the looseness of party discipline has gone too far for good government. A capable reporter, Richard L. Strout, made an analysis of 57 record votes in the House during the 78th and 79th Congresses. These were party votes on party issues. Mr. Strout, reporting the result in his column in the *Christian Science Monitor,* found that in the 57 votes, 36 Democrats—more than 15 per cent—voted with the Republicans. "They were elected as Democrats, but on key votes they voted Republican."

On the other hand, he found that there were 10 Republicans who generally voted with the Democrats. Thus 46 of the House members voted more frequently with the opposing party than with the one under whose banner they were elected. He found that an additional 155 members were so uncertain that they frequently voted with the opposing party. This is an odd situation. It means that the party in power in Congress is frequently blocked from carrying through its program. It is an unhealthy situation because the voter can have no assurance that his party will be able to put into effect its platform pledges. Unless the difficulty is remedied, there may have to be a realignment of parties or party responsibility may break down completely.

This appraisal indicates that the problem is much more acute on the Democratic side of the aisles in the Senate and House. It has been so for many years. There may be fundamental philosophical political differences between Southern Democrats and Northern Democrats. That explains part of the difficulty, but not all of it by any means. Some members of both parties are elected on local and not national issues, and therefore feel little responsibility to go along with their party. But the chief reason party lines are not more clearly drawn on the Democratic side is the failure to settle differences before an issue reaches the floor—failure to use the caucus.

Perhaps the Democrats have for so long abandoned the caucus as a means of binding the party that they would do well to start using it again without asking that Caucus Rule 7 be invoked to bind the membership. A meeting on May 26, 1946, sustains this conclusion. On that day, House Majority Whip—now Senator—John Sparkman of Alabama gave a dinner at the Statler Hotel in Washington. Twenty-eight House Democrats were present, including all of the fifteen Assistant Whips.

After dinner the British loan was discussed. Representatives Mike Monroney of Oklahoma, Willis Robertson of Virginia, and Sparkman, who had made thorough studies of the loan proposal, spoke briefly in favor of its approval. A vigorous discussion followed. Many questions were asked. Objections were answered. Party benefits were pointed out. An informal poll taken after the meeting revealed that 26 of the 28 present definitely intended to vote for the loan. One member was undecided. Another said he regretted he had already written in some letters that he was opposed to the loan and could not retract his commitments. Several members said they came to the meeting in doubt but they no longer had reason for apprehension.

Those attending this meeting were a good cross-section of the party. The same thing could have been done on a larger scale by all of the Democratic members. If the leadership feels that caucuses cannot be held because of the fear of an effort to bind the party under Rule 7, then it should ask for the elimination of Rule 7. The chief value of the caucus is a full and free discussion of the issue and an explanation of the party's stand. If a member has an honest contrary conviction, he will vote that conviction regardless of whether his party binds itself, so Rule 7 is, in fact, of doubtful value. We submit, however, that continued efforts should be made by the House Democrats to caucus, and we believe they would be successful.

Turning next to other caucus functions and party machinery in Congress, how do the parties organize to assume leadership, on the one hand, and the position of "loyal opposition" on the other?

A day or so before a new Congress comes into being (January 3rd in odd-numbered years), the members, old and newly elected, attend their respective party meetings in Washington. In the House, each group first elects caucus officers and then gets down to the more serious business of nominating a candidate for Speaker and the lesser House officers. The majority party nominates a member to be Majority Leader. The minority party candidate for Speaker automatically becomes floor leader for his side. The Democrats have one other important function—to nominate members who will serve on the important House Ways and Means Committee; the Democratic members of this committee make the other committee selections for the party. The procedures in the Senate are about parallel to those of the House, except that under the Constitution the presiding officer of the Senate is the Vice-President of the United States.

Too often these opening party conferences are sterile. Since there is no discussion of issues, the usual result is that a slate of candidates, handpicked by the party elders in the respective houses and parties, is nominated as fast as it can be gaveled through. Freshman members may be a little dazed at the speed, but the rigid seniority system is functioning on these occasions, with merit and logic playing a very small second fiddle.

There are exceptions, of course. Bitter contests have occurred in choosing a Speaker and these have at times delayed the actual organization of the House. In 1839 it took two weeks to elect a Speaker. In 1849, sixty-three ballots were taken before any candidate received even a plurality. Even as late as 1923 an insurgent movement against readopting the rules of the previous Congress delayed the election of a Speaker for two days.

In 1919 Representative Frederick H. Gillette and Representative James R. Mann opposed one another in the Republician conference for nomination as Speaker. Representative Mann was the member directly in line, since he had been the Republican floor leader in the preceding Congress. But Mr. Gillette was nominated in the conference over Representative Mann and was elected Speaker. The reason given by the Republicans for passing over Mann was that he had been too dictatorial and commanding as Minority Leader. However, this action was an exception to the rule.

The nearest thing to a Democratic contest at the beginning of the 79th Congress was the nomination of both Representative Clinton P. Anderson of New Mexico and Representative H. Streett Baldwin of Maryland for one place on the Ways and Means Committee. Ballots were used and Mr. Anderson won.

At noon on January 3rd, the brand-new Congress assembles. In the House the Clerk has his brief moment before the spotlight as he presides and calls the roll of all names certified by governors of the respective states as having been elected in their states. This call of the temporary roll produces a quorum, and the two parties nominate their condidates for Speaker. On a roll call, the majority party man wins. Only rarely in history have party lines been violated in the election of a Speaker. Even the sometimes badly split Democratic members show an unbroken phalanx in the Senate and House on these occasions.

The Speaker takes his oath, administers the oaths to his colleagues, and the House proceeds to elect the remaining officers, voting again being on straight party lines. These officers take their oaths, and then the House of Representatives formally notifies the President and the Senate it is ready to do business. The Senate goes through similar formalities, and a new session of Congress is underway.

As a preliminary to discussion of reorganization of the committee structure, it is pertinent to describe how members of committees are selected. The Republicans have much the better system, in our opinion. The ratio of majority and minority members follows substantially the proportionate representation of the two parties in the House. Third-party members usually are assigned to the minority, unless they express a preference to the contrary and vote for the majority candidate for Speaker.

Prior to the first GOP conference, the Republican delegation from each state holds a meeting and picks a member to serve on the GOP Committee on Committees. Thus, if one or more Republicans has been elected from, say, forty-one states there will be forty-one members of this group. Each member of the Committee on Committees has as many votes as there are Republican members in the House from his state. The GOP conference ratifies these selections.

In the opening Democratic caucus, the members selected for the Ways and Means Committee become by custom the Democratic Committee on Committees. A second caucus is held to ratify the assignments made by this group. The 79th Congress procedure was normal; this is what happened. After considerable preliminary discussion, Chairman Robert L. Doughton of North Carolina recommended that all the Democratic members of the previous Congress retain the same committee positions in which they had served in that Congress, except where, by request, a different arrangement was to be made. Vacancies on the various committees were filled from the newly elected members.

The day after the caucuses the recommendations of both party groups are presented to the House, and as a matter of form are agreed to without debate.

This is the way members get their committee assignments. We feel that the Republican method is fairer, more apt to represent a party truly, because it gives equitable representation of party members on the House committees. It is more democratic. The Democratic members of the Ways and Means Committee are reappointed to their positions as a matter of course if they have been reelected. If that group becomes too conservative, or if it develops a prejudice against the members from a particular section, there is no practical way the resulting injustice can be remedied. In the case of the Republican Committee on Committees, a state delegation can, at any time it wishes, select a new member to represent that state on the committee. This course comes closer to ensuring that committee assignments will be made in accordance with the prevailing philosophy and sentiment of the party.

Under the Democratic system a member of the Ways and Means Committee may be the only Democrat in the House from a particular state. On the other hand, a populous state with several Democratic members may not have a representative on the Ways and Means Committee. The number of Democrats from various states fluctuates from Congress to Congress. Manifestly it seems somewhat unfair, and it is doubtful if the will of the majority is followed when this disproportionate representation persists. Furthermore, since there are only ten minority members on the Ways and Means Committee, only a small number of states having Democratic members in the House can at the present time be represented in the making of committee assignments. A Democratic member of the Ways and Means Committee is supposed to see that his state and those in his section have proper representation. As a result of pressure placed upon him to take care of Democratic members in his *own* state, he may not be able adequately to look after the just interests and rights of the members of another state in the same section.

In the Senate, the Republican Committee on Committees consists of eight members. They are elected at the beginning of each new Congress by the party conference. A slate of names is proposed, and nominations may be made from the floor. The committee is composed of party members who have had legislative experience in the Senate. It proposes the assignment of Republican senators to the various committees. The conference usually accepts the recommendations of the committee.

The assignment of Democratic senators to committees is controlled by a committee which is a continuing committee. Vacancies are filled by the chairman of the party caucus. The Democratic committee consists of twelve members.

With fewer than one-fourth as many members to assign to committees, the task would seem to be much simpler in the Senate than in the House, but problems of seniority make it a difficult one.

The floor leaders bear the heaviest load of party responsibility in the day-to-day operations of the Senate and House. Majority Leaders are charged with preparing the legislative program and keeping it on schedule. That is too much responsibility for a single man, and would be dealt with better by policy committees. In the House, the Majority Leader must work closely with the Rules Committee because this powerful body is a bottleneck through which all major legislation must pass to reach the House floor.

The floor leaders are party agents. They ignore the desires of the individual member to the enhancement of the party's cause. Of course, they are responsible to the individual members of their party, because they are nominated and elected by the party caucus every two years. But in party government, the member soon reconciles himself to the fact that individual desires must be subordinated to the party's will. The Majority Leader has to remain on the floor continuously to see that the program is carried out to the party's satisfaction. The Minority Leader stays on the floor to defend the rights of the minority members. He gives close attention to all proposed legislation. His party expects him to be vigilant in seeing that his party's rights and principles are defended. He speaks for his party. Usually, but not invariably, the position of party leader is next in line to the Speakership.

No discussion of party government would be complete without mentioning the Whips. The Republican Whip is selected by the Committee on Committees with the approval of the conference. The Minority Whip, at this time a Democrat, is selected by the Minority Leader. The Whips appoint assistants, strategically allocated, to expedite the canvassing of each party's membership to obtain opinions or pass out information. On the Democratic side, they have to do much of the work that should be accomplished in caucus. The Whips, through their assistants, ascertain the sentiment of party members toward various pending bills. In this way they can keep their leaders informed of the votes to be expected from their party for or against proposals. The Whips also see that all members of their party are informed of the party's position on bills and amendments thereto. They keep their party members posted as to the legislative program. In the event a member wishes to leave Washington for a few days, he usually checks with his Whip to determine whether legislative business of importance will be taken up in the interval. When a vote on an important amendment to a bill is about to be taken, the Whip organizations notify all of their members to come to the floor to vote.

Both parties have Steering Committees in the Senate and House. At present the House Republican Steering Committee is selected by the party conference. The floor leader is chairman. The House Democratic Steering Committee is composed of the Minority Leader, the chairman of the caucus, and one representative from each of the fifteen districts into which, for party purposes, the country is divided.

These committees are potentially very important bodies. They constitute the executive committees of the caucus or conference. They have the continuing responsibility of watching legislative developments and of seeing that the will of the caucus or conference is carried out. They have wide discretionary powers in making decisions from day to day with respect to party action.

This is how the Steering Committees are *supposed* to operate, and the Republican committees do function in this manner in both houses. The Senate GOP group meets once a week. But when the Democratic party was in power, its Steering Committee simply did not steer. It seldom, if ever, met. Few Democratic members even knew who composed the committee. There was no caucus policy for it to effectuate. The result was that the major burden of policy decision, and of dealing with day-by-day developments, fell on the party leaders.

The solution is to abolish the Steering Committees and substitute joint majority and minority policy committees. The joint majority committee—we refer to it as the National Legislative Policy Committee—would consist of the twenty-six chairmen of the thirteen committees we recommend for each house, plus the Speaker of the House, the President of the Senate, the Majority Leaders, and the party Whips. The minority policy committee would consist of the ranking minority members of the same committees, the Minority Leaders, and the Minority Whips. This would place the responsibility of "steering" the program, and the opposition, in the hands of the members who have the power to steer.

This plan would make for coordination between caucus action, committee action, and congressional results—three factors essential in order to have effective party government and responsibility in both houses of Congress.

CHAPTER 9

Fewer — But Better Committees

Nowhere was confusion more compounded than in the haphazard committee structure of Congress before the passage of the Reorganization Act of 1946. The one hundred assorted regular, special, and joint units of the Senate and House resembled just that many isolated bastions behind which were entrenched patronage, privilege—and inefficiency. The Joint Committee on Organization logically called the streamlining of this hodgepodge the "Number one problem to be faced in any attempt to modernize and strengthen Congress." With equal force, its report commented that "Congress can no longer afford the luxury and waste of manpower and time in maintaining thirty-three standing committees of the Senate and forty-eight standing committees of the House" . . . to say nothing of the many special groups which in 1946 brought the total number of committees to ninety-six.

The most significant contribution made by the Reorganization Act to the efficiency of Congress was the *partial* overhauling of the committee system. Further improvements should and could have been made. Arguments of standpatters who invoke the weight of tradition, in the absence of more substantial objections, already have been refuted on preceding pages in the review of the countless changes Congress has made in its committees during the one hundred fifty-eight years of its existence. This history emphasizes that there has been no fixed pattern or policy in the development of the committee structure of the respective houses. Like Topsy, they "just growed." Consequently, there is nothing sacrosanct or final about their number or functions.

At all times, Congress has regarded its committees as its legislative tools, often changing their names or duties to serve current needs. Indeed, if history and precedent are good arguments, then they are on the side of change, for the record portrays a continuous practice of revamping the committees to make them serve the needs of changing conditions.

None of these observations is intended to disparage the importance of the committee system. Its usefulness and necessity increase with each forward cycle in the social, political, and technological progress of this country. We seek only to improve the system. Structurally, its chief faults, recognized by the La Follette-Monroney act, have been twofold: First, there simply have been too many committees, resulting in inevitable waste and duplication; Second, there has been no plan for meshing the work of the individual units into the majority party's program so as to permit a broad, coordinated legislative attack upon the major problems facing any given session of Congress.

Why, before the recent reorganization, were there forty-two Senate and fifty-four House committees plus a half-dozen joint groups? There are several answers. Up to the turn of the century, a member of Congress had to be chairman of a committee in order to obtain a private office. Otherwise, he met his constituents in the lobbies and foyers of the Capitol or at his hotel, and transacted his business in the corridors or in his living room. A chairmanship thus greatly enhanced his prestige and was of immense practical advantage. With the occupancy in 1908 of the old House Office Building, followed later by the more modern Senate and new House Office Buildings, all on Capitol Hill, this physical condition no longer exists. But the prestige and the prized patronage privileges of a chairmanship remain.

Even the committee rooms remaining within the Capitol building still are much coveted. Many a bitter personal vendetta has raged over their possession. The press, and later the radio, had to wage skillful campaigns to get enough space in the Capitol to report adequately the sessions of the Senate and House. In fact, somebody had to die—the beloved Colonel Edwin A. Halsey, Secretary of the Senate—before the Senate Rules Committee could make a shift and install the broadcast booths that now serve the upper chamber. Leslie Biffle, who replaced Halsey, relinquished an office too large for the new Assistant Secretary's needs, and the radio correspondents took it over. Television and facsimile will bring new space problems.

Certain committees arose from particular investigations, and some were the result of reforms. Still others were created to give the majority party effective whips for its program. The important fact is that these committees were inherited from the last major changes of earlier Congresses and that they were unsuited to discharge the greatly increased and more complex work of the Congresses of today and tomorrow.

Excellent studies and recommendations have been made as to the proper number of committees each chamber needs to operate efficiently. Among them, we mention former Senator La Follette's strong case for reducing the Senate's thirty-three regular units to thirteen. After some compromises, the Joint Committee on Organization adopted his basic plan but increased the total to fifteen. Representative Everett M. Dirksen of Illinois, another member of the La Follette-

Monroney group, recommended slashing the standing House units from forty-eight to fifteen. Representative James W. Wadsworth of New York, who had previously served two terms in the Senate, proposed a House reorganization that would leave the number at seventeen. The Wadsworth plan, with two additions, became the plan accepted by Congress.

Under the Reorganization Act, some of the Senate and House committees are matched so as to have identical functions. Some of them are not. Sound administration requires that *the same number of committees exist in both bodies and that they have identical functions.* This would facilitate combined hearings and provide for an easy exchange of ideas and information. While recognizing that the reduction of Senate committees from 33 to 15 and of House committees from 48 to 19 was a major accomplishment, we believe that the best plan for setting up a true parallel system was the original one worked out by Dr. George B. Galloway, staff director of the Joint Committee. He proposed to abolish a number of committees and merge the rest into thirteen in each house. Each of these thirteen would deal with a broad area of public policy, with jurisdiction indicated as follows:

Proposed Committees	*Agency Jurisdiction*
1. Agriculture	Department of Agriculture
2. Commerce	Department of Commerce
	Federal Trade Commission
	Tariff Commission
3. Labor	Department of Labor
	National Labor Relations Board
4. Foreign Affairs	State Department
5. National Defense	War Department
	Navy Department
	Coast Guard
6. Fiscal Policy	Treasury Department
	Federal Reserve System
	Bureau of the Budget
	Federal Loan Agency
	Federal Deposit Insurance Corporation
	Securities and Exchange Commission

Proposed Committees	Agency Jurisdiction
7. General [1] Welfare	National Housing Agency
	Federal Security Agency
	Office of Education
	Public Health Service
	Railroad Retirement Board
	Veterans Administration
8. Natural Resources	Interior Department
	Tennessee Valley Authority
	Federal Power Commission
	Federal Communications Commission
	Rural Electrification Administration [2]
9. Judiciary	Department of Justice
10. Civil Service	Post Office Department
	U.S. Employees Compensation Commission
	Civil Service Commission
11. Public Works	Federal Works Agency
12. Transportation	Interstate Commerce Commission
	Civil Aeronautics Authority
	Maritime Commission
	Public Roads Administration
	Inland Waterways Corporation
13. Administrative	General Accounting Office
	Government Printing Office
	Library of Congress
	National Archives

---

[1] Changed by authors from Social to General Welfare.
[2] Added by the authors.

The above is by no means a complete outline of the Galloway plan, but here are a few outstanding features that appeal to us particularly.

Responsibility for raising tax money and spending it would be centralized in a single Fiscal Policy Committee in each house. For years, hardworking subcommittees of the powerful House Appropriations group have ground out the budget bills for the various departments. They trimmed here, expanded there, and did their best to check the natural tendencies of bureaucracy to feed on itself. In the past decade the total federal appropriations reported out have leaped from less than eight billions to a staggering peak of over one hundred billions in 1945.

No one expected that a war could be fought on a pay-as-you-go fiscal policy. But it is debatable whether or not a larger share of the war costs could not have been raised from taxes, instead of saddling the government and taxpayers of this and future generations with $121,000,000,000 in relatively high interest-bearing war bonds. However, the Appropriations Committee was and still is, for practical purposes, isolated from the House Ways and Means Committee, where all tax legislation must originate. One of the achievements of the Reorganization Act is the provision for a legislative budget which requires the fixing of the maximum amount to be appropriated each year. The act provides that the taxing and spending committees shall meet jointly at the beginning of each session and prepare a legislative budget by February 15th. If the estimated receipts exceed the estimated expenditures they shall recommend a reduction in the public debt. If they find that more will be spent than received, they shall submit for adoption by Congress a resolution that the public debt should be increased to take care of the deficiency. But these well-intentioned provisions are of little value because there are no means of enforcing them. The only effective way that receipts and expenditures can be balanced is to vest the money-raising and spending powers in some one committee such as proposed. Yet the mere fact that Congress has taken a partial step toward controlling federal expenditures is a promising indication that real budget control is close at hand.

Often during the war the Appropriations Committee was confronted with a multi-billion-dollar deficiency or emergency request for funds. These vast sums were voted after as much study of their proposed use as time permitted. We do not criticize these actions. There was a war to be won. Our point is that if this same committee also had had the responsibility of trying to make ends meet and books balance in the federal treasury, every time it voted out a ten-billion-dollar appropriation there would have been an incentive, if not the clear duty, to prod the subcommittee dealing with revenue into digging up more tax dollars.

Poll after poll indicated that the American people were willing to shoulder a much heavier tax burden than the timid House Ways and Means and the Senate Finance Committees ever asked them to bear. During the entire period of suddenly vastly expanded government spending, the committees charged with raising the money lagged behind public opinion and the hard fiscal facts of life of a nation at war. Channeling this divided responsibility into one Fiscal Policy Committee would act as a remedy to prevent an already dangerous situation from getting worse, and substitute careful fiscal stewardship for bungling.

Whether or not a true merger of the armed services is voted by the present or some future Congress, the logic of pooling legislative brains and resources in the field of national defense, as provided in the Reorganization Act, is so sound as to put a difficult burden of proof on those who defend the system of separate military and naval affairs committees in both chambers. The mammoth greenish plume that shot eight miles into the air over Alamogordo, New Mexico, in July, 1945, and later over Hiroshima and Nagasaki, created national and international problems far beyond the scope of any individual branch of the service. The expensive duplication of radar research that was revealed when the Army "won" the race to contact the moon is but another example of the wisdom of Congress in providing for single committee scrutiny of military and naval affairs.

Most major changes in the military services require legis

lation. One cannot help but wonder how much duplication and inefficiency in the last war would have been avoided if the various plans and requests of the Army and Navy had been threshed out before one single committee in each house charged with responsibility for the entire field of national defense. The bitter jealousy that now finds one service or the other trying to "beat somebody to the punch" with a particular piece of legislation loses much of its substance when that measure passes through a single committee composed of men familiar with both services. The net result of amalgamation should be a much better coordinated policy. Legislation should be truly national, rather than reflecting the philosophy of a particular service group.

The Committee on the Organization of Congress recommended that the Claims and District of Columbia Committees of both houses be abolished. Congress followed the committee report on the abolition of the Claims Committees. Under the Tort Claims Act passed by Congress, as previously noted, claims up to $1000 can be settled by the federal agency involved. Demands for larger amounts are tried by U.S. District Courts, sitting without a jury. We fear, however, that the limitations and exceptions contained in this act may still require Congress to handle many claims. It is our view that Congress should have made a clean break with all claims, excepting those governmental corporations which the Supreme Court has held can be sued as a private person.

Concerning claims against the government, the old system not only was tremendously wasteful and costly, but in too many instances did not provide just redress for the complaining citizen. If his case was presented by an influential member of Congress, and if the claim-bill calendar was not too crowded, and if the penny-pinchers happened to be off the floor for a moment, a well-deserving person might have obtained a fair or good allowance. But this was the exception rather than the rule. The faults of the old system were glaringly illustrated whenever a news story turned up some person living in poverty whose whole life might have been changed had his just claim against Uncle Sam been granted years before, when first presented.

Consider the case of Charles R. Hooper, now eighty, who lost an eye while working for the federal government in the Navy Yard in 1894. For nearly fifty years he has been pressing his claim against the government. Six times it passed Congress and each time it failed to receive presidential approval.

It is exceedingly unfortunate that Congress did not follow the recommendation of its joint committee by giving self-rule to the District of Columbia, and simultaneously doing away with the District Committees. The manner in which Congress attempts to govern the District of Columbia is indefensible. The nearly one million residents of Washington are in the same category as felons, aliens, incompetents, and federally supported Indians. This fact once led George Allen, one-time District Commissioner and later a top adviser to President Truman, to hire a whole tribe of Indians and put on a colorful demonstration at a Democratic National Convention in an effort to bring party pressure to bear to grant full citizenship to the people who live in the nation's capital.

These citizens pay local and federal taxes at rates exceeding those of many states. In the fiscal year of 1946 they raised almost $48,000,000 from local sources to support the city government. But they have no voice in the spending of this tax money. Taxation without representation was one of the things that made Americans fight the Revolution. These Washingtonians perform all obligations of citizenship, jury service, full responsibilities under Selective Service, and so on, but they are foreigners as far as the basic right to control their own destiny is concerned.

From the congressional viewpoint, membership on the Senate and House District of Columbia Committees is a thankless job and a positive political liability. It brings no cheers from a member's constituents. On the contrary, there are quite a few ex-members who assert that their defeats were due in large part to their efforts to do a conscientious job on a District Committee. Almost every senator or congressman who has served on these groups can testify that his opponents have made effective use of the situation. Therefore a vacancy, especially in the chairmanship, goes begging. During the 79th Congress when Senator Pat McCarran of Nevada moved up to the chairmanship of the Judiciary Committee, the next senators in line to head the District group ran like frightened hares to the nearest legislative refuge until the loquacious Bilbo of Mississippi was reached. The latter promptly accepted, to the almost unanimous dismay of the local citizenry.

Many issues important to Washington city have to be decided by telephone polls of the Senate District Committee because its members, busy with more important national problems, just cannot spare the time to attend committee meetings. The net result ranges from lackadaisical to mediocre. The great city, despite its outward beauty, has for years contained some of the most horrible slums in the nation, slums within sight of the inspiring dome of the Capitol. Public services now taken for granted in many municipalities, such as a modern jail or juvenile court system, to name but two, lag pitifully in the District of Columbia. The city is neglected as an orphan and treated like the proverbial stepchild. The blame rests squarely on Congress. Frequent exposures of bad management in District institutions reveal an unfortunate lack of consideration by Congress for the inhabitants of what is now the most important capital city in the world.

The solution is at hand. Appropriate bills have long been pending. While always retaining adequate power to legislate on federal matters pertaining to the city and to establish federal institutions anywhere within its boundaries, Congress should unburden itself of the local housekeeping. District residents should be given the right to vote, elect their own officials, participate in national elections, and be represented in Congress. They had the right of local self-government seventy-five years ago, but it was at the sufferance of Congress. When some local extravagance developed, Congress promptly abolished the voting privilege.

In view of the fact that the District government would act at times on matters affecting the federal government, all such legislation should be of a provisional nature. Designated subcommittees of the suggested Senate and House Administrative Committees could be assigned the task of reviewing such local legislation. Likewise, a designated District official should have a liaison office on Capitol Hill. This executive would perform valuable service in handling complaints that often are trivial, but which members cannot afford to ignore.

The amount of work to be eliminated on Capitol Hill by discarding the Claims and District Committees is startling, when analyzed. In the 78th Congress, more than 10,500 bills were referred to committees. *One out of every four of these 10,500 went to the Claims or District Committees.* When the bills that survived committee consideration and were reported out to the Senate and House are tabulated for this same 78th Congress, the result is even more amazing. *More than 40 per cent of all bills placed on the calendars of the respective houses were reported out by these four committees.* Here is the detailed breakdown:

78th Congress	Bills Referred	Bills Reported
SENATE		
Claims Committee	909	579
District Committee	93	52
HOUSE		
Claims Committee	1612	737
District Committee	116	42
Total for the four committees......	2730	1410
Total for ALL committees	10596	3237
PER CENT TO BE ELIMINATED UNDER PROPOSED PLAN..	25.8	43.6

As Congress has to a limited extent relieved itself of private claims under the Reorganization Act, we point out quickly that the above percentages do not mean that the total work load of Congress on claims could be decreased in that proportion. That *was* the work load, and the District housekeeping job *still* remains, and large segments of congressional machinery are *still* employed in the routine of preparation, introduction, referral, printing of bills, and hearings on District matters.

Another important advantage of a parallel system of committees remains to be emphasized.

At the present time there are three principal means by which the Senate and House act together. First, there is the old device of the conference committee to iron out differences in Senate and House versions of the same legislation. Second, there is the temporary joining of hands for a specific problem, of which examples are the Joint Committee on the Organization of Congress, and the joint committee which deals with Selective Service occupational deferment of officers and employees of the legislative branch. Third, there is a permanent form of combined endeavor in the Joint Committee on Internal Revenue Taxation, a continuing group that meets regularly. The excellent work this latter group has done demonstrates the advantage of joint action.

Under the simplified and parallel grouping of committees we advocate, congressional operation comparable to the excellent combined staff work of the American and British forces during the recent war, will become normal procedure. We are not proposing joint committees. But we do recommend that the parallel units on each side of the Capitol combine their efforts as much as possible. Business and executive meetings would be held separately in the respective committee rooms. Each committee would be free to pursue any particular inquiry in its field independently of the corresponding unit in the other chamber.

Combined sessions, however, could hear the same witnesses, see the same charts, and receive the same statement "to be incorporated in the printed record." Thus the endless repetition of testimony that now occurs year after year would be eliminated, with great savings in time, records, tempers, and taxpayers' money.

With all committees competently staffed, each of the parallel bodies on occasion might assign some of its experts to do joint research or lay the groundwork for a joint inquiry. We are not naive enough to think any reorganization is going to change human nature. There always will be the temptation for a committee to keep a hot investigation in its own bailiwick so it can enjoy the radio and press spotlight. But if a streamlined Congress, working more closely together, will use the combined-staff technique that is available, it will obviate the need for many expensive and lengthy special investigations, frequently by newly created special committees, that now are undertaken. This also would abate greatly the rivalries that sometimes arise between the Senate and House when such probes are in progress.

Whenever differences exist between the Senate and House on pending legislation, how much more logical it will be to refer the matter to the proper subcommittees of the proposed parallel committees. They will have worked together previously during hearings on the issue in question, and since each will have used the same permanent committee staffs, most of the Senate-House differences that now arise should cease to exist. The present conference committee system, dating back to 1789, often results in a prolonged tug-of-war between the two houses. The battle in the 79th Congress over the so-called "full employment" bill was an excellent example. We believe the simpler, more effective machinery outlined here will enable the two chambers to iron out their differences much more quickly, and will mark another progressive step in making Congress a more efficient political instrument.

We come now to the capstone of this streamlined committee structure—the establishment of a National Legislative Policy Committee as an integral part of the legislative machinery. When the Budget and Accounting Act was passed in 1921, Congress and the Executive for the first time were provided with a financial chart showing where the country was and where it was going. This was expanded by provisions for a legislative budget, and also the expenditure analysis of executive agencies by the Comptroller General under the Reorganization Act of 1946. These provisions only relate to budget and expenditure, which are only a part of the legislative picture. Prior to this, as far as finances were concerned, Congress was like a ship sailing without chart or compass. It just floundered around in financial confusion.

Many of the benefits from these progressive steps are nullified, however, by lack of any adequate means of keeping a perspective of the entire legislative program before the Congress and the people. Even under the new rules, tax laws may lag sadly behind commitments for appropriations. During the past two decades, calculations of both the Ways and

Means and the Finance Committees and of the Appropriations Committees often have gone awry completely because, late in the session, Congress adopted some major national program without considering sufficiently its effect on the nation's fiscal policy.

Legislative policy generally is in about the same helpless condition as was fiscal planning prior to 1921. Congress theoretically is responsible for the "state of the union." Actually, legislation often drifts about in a sea of party politics, selfish interest, parliamentary maneuvering—and chance. With so many duties to perform and committee sessions to attend, the average member is intimately acquainted only with the work of his own assignments.

Likewise, committee chairmen are so occupied with the immediate tasks before them that they have little time to become well versed in the entire legislative history that relates to their particular work. They have even less time to work closely with the other committee chairmen. The result is confusion, lack of coordination, lack of any overall picture of where Congress is heading at the moment. We wish to point up the need for a National Legislative Policy Committee to do for all areas of public policy what the Budget Act did for national finances.

Naturally, members of the Republican party, since it is now the party in power, should make up this very important committee. But it goes almost without recording that the Democratic party should set up a parallel policy committee of its own, to watch carefully and criticize, as is the traditional function of the opposition. Both the Democratic party and the GOP perform this function now in a haphazard sort of way. There are Steering Committees, and occasional caucuses, but they vary widely in influence and importance from session to session. We believe that making the suggested committee an official organ of the Congress will greatly strengthen party responsibility, something that is needed badly in this country's political system. This factor alone would add much to the efficiency of the legislative and executive branches of government.

The Joint Committee on the Organization of Congress, after considering the advice of many of its members and leading political scientists, recommended the establishment of majority and minority policy committees, four in all. These would consist of seven members from the majority and minority parties of each house, and function separately in each body. The recommendation was approved by the Senate. But part of the price of passage of the Reorganization bill in the House was the striking out of this basic provision.

The Senate, after the House rejected the policy committee proposal, made a temporary arrangement for policy committees of its own. By means of an amendment to an appropriation bill, $30,000 was allotted for staff and administration of a majority and a minority policy committee, consisting of seven members each. This was only for the first six months of 1947, unless renewed. It will be seen from the foregoing that even the policy committees which were approved by the Senate and killed in the House were too limited in scope to be really effective.

The National Legislative Policy Committee should be a joint Senate-House group consisting of the Vice-President or President pro tempore of the Senate, the Speaker of the House, the Majority Leaders and their Whips, and the thirteen committee chairmen from each house. The entire group, under the simplified committee plan proposed here, would not exceed thirty-five, and thus not be unwieldy. We do not hold with some advocates of congressional reorganization that such a group should meet regularly with the President and his Cabinet. The prospect of the committee's journeying down to the White House every Monday morning strikes us as inefficient and not conducive to the best relations between the executive and legislative branches. We do think that the White House assistants assigned to liaison work on Capitol Hill should meet with this policy group, however, as frequently as determined by the committee.

A full-time staff of highly trained civil service legislative assistants and clerks should be provided. In the present situation, with the Republicans controlling the Senate and House, and the Democrats controlling the executive department, majority and minority policy committees could serve as a basis for the working relationship so imperative when there is divided control. They could do this by bringing the majority and minority parties together to agree, in so far as possible, on a bipartisan program. When control is divided, the minority policy committee still advises the President, so it might be expected that the President would approve any legislative program agreed upon by the committees.

There would be three definite and vital functions assigned to the National Legislative Policy Committee. It should first completely and critically examine past and existing legislation, and outline for Congress a suitable course of action based on current needs of the nation. This very process would result additionally in more comprehensive study from a national viewpoint of the plans of action advanced by the Executive. Second, from both studies the committee would prepare the necessary schedule of legislation to carry out what it considered the most feasible program. Third, the committee would follow through on this schedule with committees of both houses, and the departments and agencies, in order to report to Congress and to the people on how the national legislative policy was being effectuated, together with suggestions for amendments or corrective measures where necessary.

Such a course of action would tend to correct the unique

and almost unfair advantage which the President usually enjoys. He and his advisers work feverishly for weeks to put into shape a program they think will best meet the current problems facing the nation. Obviously, being human, they cannot escape placing the executive branch in the most favorable light possible, often at the expense of the Congress. This program goes up to the Capitol with much fanfare. Frequently it is broadcast on all networks. It is printed in full in many newspapers and publications, and all papers carry complete digests. The public hears it, sees it, and has something tangible to mull over and evaluate. And what from Congress? Usually a series of strictly partisan statements that manage to make the end of the broadcast, or the inside pages of the newspapers.

Under our plan, the President's recommendations are placed in their proper perspective. The National Legislative Policy Committee would go to work immediately on the annual executive "state of the union" message. It would formulate its own version of national needs, including rebuttal to any implied accusations made by the Executive. The committee could inject issues that were omitted, intentionally or otherwise, from the presidential message. Then Congress would assemble in joint session to hear the most persuasive speaker in the ranks of the majority make the committee's report, with a reasonable time allotted to a spokesman for the minority. Congress would thus assert its legislative supremacy and have its "day at the bar," before the public. Its own state of the union message might soon rank in importance, prestige, and public interest with the annual statement from the White House.

Aside from the not-to-be-discounted showmanship involved, the work of this top committee should show a complete legislative trial balance sheet. All the activities of the party in power would be directed toward common predetermined goals with which the people would be acquainted. The committees and all the legislative and executive units would be charged with the responsibility for carrying out a carefully planned program, and not drift around, sometimes bitterly antagonistic to each other, as is the fact today.

Chapter 10

Seniority, Sectionalism, and Senility

Much of the progress that will be achieved by modernizing the committee structure of Congress might easily be lost if at the same time certain improvements are not made in the procedures and conduct of these congressional units. Foremost among present evils is the ancient and rigid seniority system that governs the selection of committee chairmen and determines rank in almost every other phase of group activity in the national legislature.

Under this system, the member of the party in power who has served the longest on any given committee is for practical purposes the *only* person eligible for the chairmanship of that committee, regardless of his qualifications, physical fitness, or any other factor that might be weighed, or any other method of trying to pick the best person for the post.

The minority party follows the same rule with slavish devotion. When there is a change in party control, the member who, while in the minority, had the greatest tenure, moves into the chairmanship. Thus at the beginning of the 80th Congress Democratic chairmen had to abdicate in favor of Republican chairmen, who took over on the same seniority principle. True, there was the formality of an election when the 80th Congress was organized. But it was only a formality. Any member who tried to buck the system on any such occasion would be howled down as an upstart or maverick and probably subjected to such political punishment as denial of patronage. It has happened.

This much can be said in favor of rule by seniority: the law of averages works in its favor. In many cases, because of knowledge and skill acquired during years of grappling with problems that regularly come before his committee, the man who is handed the chairmanship through seniority in most cases would be chosen for the post by any system of more democratic election that might be devised. But there is abundant evidence to prove that fitness and leadership are not based upon years in office alone. We will cite one or two examples that dramatize the inherent danger of the system, and that can be spelled out without reflecting in any way upon any present member of the Senate or House.

When a vacancy occurs and there happen to be two men on a committee who took their oath of office at the same time, the seniority system resorts to the alphabet to determine who shall be chairman. When Congressman Edward Taylor of Colorado died, there were two members who could claim the chairmanship of the important House Appropriations Committee: Representative Clifton A. Woodrum of Virginia and Representative Clarence Cannon of Missouri. Both had served with distinction. Mr. Cannon's skill in handling budget matters was exceptional. Mr. Woodrum had become one of the recognized leaders of the House whose advice carried weight on both sides of the aisle. Representative Cannon got the chairmanship because his name began with *C*, which ranks far ahead of *W* in the alphabet. The noted Scripps-Howard columnist, Thomas L. Stokes, Jr., made this comment in recalling the incident when, during the 79th Congress, Mr. Woodrum retired:

"This bit of monkey business shows how silly the seniority system is without going into the qualifications of the two

men. *Neither the committee itself, nor the House, had anything to say about the chairmanship of this most important
committee, nor do they for any others.*[1] A man moves up on
the committee list through the years and automatically becomes chairman when he gets to the top, whatever his
abilities. In this case of rival claims, the alphabet was invoked."

By the same method of alphabetical selection, former Representative Andrew J. May of Kentucky headed the House
Military Affairs Committee in recent years because *M* comes
before *T*. Representative Robert Ewing Thomason of Texas
had exactly the same length of service, but there was no opportunity to choose between the two. On the Senate side,
few, if any, members had a record of more distinguished
public service than the late Senator Carter Glass of Virginia.
It is nevertheless true that he retained his important post
as chairman of the Senate Appropriations Committee although physically unable even to attend a session of the
Senate, or of his committee, for more than three years.

There was a potentially dangerous situation in the Senate
at the outbreak of World War II, when former Senator
Robert R. Reynolds of North Carolina headed the Military
Affairs Committee. Senator Reynolds held widely voiced
views that were directly opposed to the policy and course of
action upon which the country and the Congress had agreed.
But seniority had put him there and only death or retirement could take him away. The Senate was helpless to do
anything about the situation. The senator in question retired, but not until the war was nearly over. This is too much
of a chance to take with the prestige and efficiency of a
branch of the government already in a dangerously low
state. A hostile chairman has in times past, and may again at
any unpredictable moment in the future, impede a very vital

---

[1] These, and all italics hereinafter, supplied by the authors.

and constructive part of the congressional program. The Legislative Reorganization Act completely omits treatment of this paramount problem.

The present Senate offers a striking example of the penalties of seniority. There are several younger members who generally are acclaimed as possessing uncommon leadership and insight in fields which today loom as second to none in deciding the future course of the country. Typical of this group are Senators Wayne Morse of Oregon, J. William Fulbright of Arkansas, Henry Cabot Lodge, Jr., of Massachusetts, Brien McMahon of Connecticut, John Sparkman of Alabama, and Edward J. Thye of Minnesota. Unless tradition is violated and the averages upset, none of these senators is likely to attain an important regular committee chairmanship until he begins his thirteenth year of consecutive service—that is to say, has been elected for a third six-year term. Senator McMahon upset precedent in the 79th Congress when he became head of the special committee to study atomic-energy control.

Another serious defect of the seniority system challenges the very character of truly representative government. Many men are returned by the voters time and time again on the record of their statesmanship and service to their respective states and districts. But no one will deny that others of lesser abilities have remained in office and advanced without undue effort or unusual ability to positions of power on Capitol Hill, because they happened to come from areas where the tradition for one particular party, plus the power of entrenched city, courthouse, and state machines, make a farce of the two-party system.

Once a member is "in," as a Democrat from the South or a Republican from the Middle West, it is relatively easy, by comparison with more politically sensitive sections of the country, to remain in office. In the South, the question of constitutional rights of a large minority and the operation of a poll tax have served to limit the electorate to in some cases as few as ten per cent of the potential voting population. Without reflecting personally on any individual, it seems pertinent to observe the House Rules Committee roster in the 79th Congress. This committee is the most powerful unit in either House or Senate, controlling the priority of all bills that are to be taken up in the lower chamber. Of the eight Democratic members, five were from the South, while all four Republican members were from the Middle West. The same disproportionate representation of particular sections of the United States ran through the entire list of committee chairmanships. The great Far West, which during the past war demonstrated its tremendous physical and economic importance to the nation, and which is increasing in population faster than any other section, was almost without a voice in the leadership of the national legislature. Likewise, as modern industrialization has made once rock-ribbed Republican New England a more closely matched political battleground, with resulting turnover in office, some important states in that area lacked proper apportionment of congressional positions of power and influence.

We offer a solution to this serious dilemma. At the beginning of each Congress, members of the majority party of each committee should elect chairmen by majority vote. Secret ballots should be used. If a chairman becomes incapacitated by reason of ill health or otherwise, a new leader for the committee should be chosen immediately in a similar manner. However, once a post is filled for a term, the chairman should not be removed except for physical incapacity or for conduct that would also disqualify him to remain a member of Congress. The minority party should follow the same procedure in allocating the posts of ranking members of the committee.

The Reorganization Act recognizes that the dictatorial powers of committee chairmen should be curbed. The act says it shall be the "duty" of the chairmen of committees to report bills promptly to the floor on any measure approved by the committee, and that "necessary steps" shall be taken to bring the bill to a vote. This adds little to the obligation a chairman of a committee has always had. We doubt if it will change the present procedure appreciably, for the reason that no easy method of enforcement is provided for in the act.

There have been cases where committee chairmen permitted overzealous investigators to violate fundamental civil rights in prosecuting investigations, and to make public reports in the name of the committee that blackened the reputations of innocent citizens who had no redress available. Members of committees in some instances have publicly denounced such actions, but, under the present system, are powerless to prevent their repetition. As a good example of this bad practice we cite the House Committee on Un-American Activities under the chairmanship of former Representative Martin Dies of Texas.

Even under the provisions of the Reorganization Act, a chairman can at many stages of the consideration of a bill in committee still exercise virtual veto powers, by "sitting on a bill" or "carrying it around in his pocket." Some years ago, when Representative Philip P. Campbell of Kansas headed the House Rules Committee, he was dubbed by his enemies the "Walking Pigeonhole," because of an alleged habit of stuffing important bills into his inside coat pocket and carrying them around until the session ended.

In the middle 'thirties a carefully considered retirement bill, aimed at making low-paid government jobs attractive to a better class of workers, passed the House. Senator William J. Bulow of South Dakota, chairman of the Senate Civil Service Committee, opposed it. All efforts to get this senator to call a committee meeting were futile. He sat on the bill for an entire session of Congress and delayed action on a measure which would have passed by an overwhelming vote both in the committee and on the floor. A chairman should be a servant, not the czar, of his committee, and these arbitrary and capricious powers must be effectively curbed by definite, effectuating provisions available to any member.

The Reorganization Act wisely provides for regular meetings of all committees, which are worked into a schedule that will permit members to attend sessions with the same regularity that businessmen show up at their favorite civic luncheon clubs. We would propose, as a fixed feature of these committee meetings, that an allocation of time be made for members to present their own bills. Upon unanimous report by the committee, we suggest that bills should be assigned automatically to the regular calendar of the Senate and House. Likewise, the request of one-third of the members should automatically discharge a bill from a committee and place it on the calendar. This would prevent a chairman from thwarting the will of his committee by delaying the reporting of a measure.

Under the general direction of the National Legislative Policy Committee, each staff would prepare for the committee's approval, early in each session, an agenda of the anticipated problems to be dealt with and time assigned to each major topic. Changes necessitated by new bills would be fitted into this program as the committee might decide. With such assignments, the chairman could hold his subcommittee chiefs to a definite schedule, and members could serve efficiently on several such groups.

There is growing dissatisfaction with the gradual increase of "star chamber" committee sessions. During the war many such closed meetings were deemed necessary as a security measure. In the public interest, the Reorganization Act provides that as a general rule all committee meetings shall be open to the public, aside from purely executive sessions. In addition, it should be mandatory that committees publish all votes on pending legislation and amendments considered, including adverse votes. A daily digest should be prepared by each committee staff for publication in the *Congressional Record,* and a monthly indexed summary should be furnished committee members. The status of pending programs would be included, as well as the roll calls referred to above. These things should be done by the staffs of the various committees rather than by the Joint Committee on Printing, as is provided in the Reorganization Act.

With the staffs taking over the routine, members will be relieved of many man-hours of work and will have more time for deliberation and discussion of policies, and to follow the work of other committees. They will also be able to take regular inspection trips to secure firsthand information on the work regularly coming under the jurisdiction of their committees. This will be criticized as more "congressional junkets," but it is well to recall that if President Truman, then senator, had not taken one such inspection trip on his own initiative, there would have been no Truman committee with its brilliant record of searching out wartime recklessness and exposing weak spots in America's war production.

The story of how the Truman committee was born shows exactly how much is left to chance. The Missourian was on the Senate Appropriations Committee and, because of his World War I experience, was particularly interested in the War Department budget. Frank McNaughton and Walter

Hehmeyer in their excellent biography, *This Man Truman,* tell what happened:

"In mid-January of 1941, Truman began to receive disturbing reports on the conduct of the national defense program. . . . Letters from Missouri complained that money was being wasted in the construction work being done at Fort Leonard Wood. The Senator decided to see for himself. He loaded his suitcases into his car and drove from Washington straight and unannounced to the fort.

"He strolled quietly through the sprawling huts and skeleton framework of the great barracks. On every hand he saw evidence of waste and poor management. Then he drove back to Washington, visiting camp construction projects along the way. Everywhere the story was the same.

"Truman returned to Washington angry clear through. On February 10, 1941, he told the Senate about it. He insisted that to avoid a national scandal and to spur on the defense effort a special committee should be established that would hunt down waste and inefficiency and open up the bottlenecks. On March 1, 1941, the Senate set up a committee of seven Senators and granted $15,000 to it. Truman was made chairman. . . .

"It is impossible to assess the accomplishments of the committee in terms of dollars and cents. Thoughtful persons have estimated that it saved between four and six billions of dollars and hundreds of thousands of lives. . . ."

Requiring members to make a complete report to their committee immediately upon their return from field trips, and having digests of these prepared by the staff and printed in the committee bulletins, would tighten up on the admitted possibility of abuse of congressional traveling.

We believe this modernized system should be all-inclusive and cover every aspect of committee work. There will be no need for additional units, special or select, as such committees are generally known. We do not set this down as iron-clad procedure. There probably will not be many occasions when a Congress is faced with such a revolutionary problem as the atom. When such cases do occur, the question of whether or not a separate group should be assigned to the job might be decided first by the National Legislative Policy Committee, subject to the approval of the Senate or House, whichever is involved. Any issue worthy of such unusual consideration should be studied jointly by both houses; this would be facilitated by the recommendations that we have made concerning parallel committees and joint action. The advisability of joint consideration in special cases is well illustrated by congressional handling of the domestic control of atomic energy. The special McMahon committee in the Senate gave the problem a thorough study, in contrast to that of the House Military Affairs Committee, which was comparatively superficial. Had a joint committee been established, both houses would have been equally well informed on the subject and the friction that resulted would have been avoided.

The next important step in improving committee work is to provide better liaison between the Capitol Hill units and the executive departments under their respective legislative jurisdiction.

CHAPTER 11

Agency-Committee Teamwork: The Need of the Hour

THE REPORT AND QUESTION PERIOD PROPOSED EARLIER IN THIS book, is in no sense the complete answer to good teamwork between the legislative and executive branches of the government. There still is a large area for improving relations between the committees of Congress and the departments and agencies over which they have legislative jurisdiction and budgetary control. The same kind of face-to-face discussions as proposed for the report and question period should become standard practice in the committees, though on a more informal and intimate basis. The war and the problems left in its wake produced many examples of lack of coordination between the legislators and administrators.

Today, Congress gets much of its information about the executive agencies through charges of irregularities. Data upon which the charges are made are obtained either from a constituent, from other members of Congress, by plodding through the thousand-page hearings on appropriation bills, from the long and often dull annual departmental reports which are from six to nine months old when distributed, through radio and press reports, or from committee exposés.

The party in power naturally wants to cover up, and the opposition party wants to condemn. Bitter but superficial and uninformed partisan debate results. The press and radio thrive on the controversy. Under-Secretary of State Dean Acheson made this point very succinctly in his testimony before the La Follette-Monroney group. Said Acheson:

"Our democracy, which is built on the division of powers, on a whole series of checks, as it goes along requires public information and public discussion which brings about an understanding of the problem, an adjustment of difficulties and agreement. We must have a very large measure of agreement in this country in order to operate.

"Now, on the contrary, what the press and radio require is controversy. It is controversy which is news, and news is controversy. Therefore, what is given to the public—and if it does not exist it has to be built up— is the fact that there is a controversy going on always of some sort. . . .

"The thing that people read is 'Senator or Congressman So-and-so flays Cabinet officer!' You read that, it is lively news. If the story is that at an amicable discussion we worked out a problem, it is not news, nobody wants to read that."

Many radio and newspaper men will take exception to this broad indictment, but the evidence seems largely on the side of Mr. Acheson. Here and there one finds exceptional commentators and columnists, men such as Lowell Mellett, formerly a top editor in the Scripps-Howard organization, who emphasized to his reporters the duty of recording the accomplishments of public servants as well as their shortcomings and bickerings. But few will question the general accuracy of Mr. Acheson's charge. It is an important fact that most of the federal agencies, quietly in many cases, through trial and error, do a remarkably good job in carrying out general congressional law. The occasional few do poorly.

In addition to the broad scope of the proposed reports on the floor of the Senate and House, the committees need three types of service from the respective departments they are charged with overseeing. First, they need periodic reports from key men in the executive agencies, and advance information on plans that involve national policy and will require further legislative action. Second, they require day-to-day liaison with the agencies to handle routine matters and provide competent coordination with committee staffs. Third, they should have a definite system for review of rules and regulations to be issued by the executive agencies in carrying out the intent of laws passed by Congress. We deal with these aspects of the problem in that order.

Excellent relations between the State Department and the foreign affairs committees of both houses resulted when Secretary of State Cordell Hull took the latter groups into his confidence on the big issues of planning for postwar world organization. The great virtue of this liaison was that Congress was informed *in advance* of the proposed program and the legislation involved. Mr. Hull and others who followed him kept the committeemen supplied with information on the progress of negotiations and related matters. The procedure also had the desirable effect of carrying out literally the constitutional provision that requires the President, in ratifying treaties, to seek the advice and consent of the Senate. In this instance, it was *advice*. Months later, *consent* was given in a surprisingly unanimous vote for adherence to the United Nations.

The President further contributed to this little-used method of executive-legislative cooperation by including members of the two foreign relations committees in the United States delegations to the San Francisco Conference, to the Mexico City meeting that produced the Pact of Chapultepec, to the organization session of the United Nations at London, to the conference of Foreign Ministers in Paris, and to the UN Assembly meeting in New York. No great differences of opinion between Congress and the Executive developed because full information was available, as well as bipartisan representation from Congress. The issue of this nation's leadership and responsibilities in world affairs was approached and has been handled on a high non-partisan basis.

There is another example of this widely acclaimed method of cooperation in a domestic field. For two years while administrator of the National Housing Agency, John B. Blandford, Jr., and his staff held informal monthly meetings with the House Public Buildings and Grounds Committee headed by Representative Fritz G. Lanham of Texas. Members of Lanham's group told the authors how useful this was from a legislator's viewpoint. Testifying before the Joint Committee on Organization, Mr. Blandford expressed the administrator's feeling in these words:

"Rather early in our career as an agency we were concerned with the infrequency and the formality of our contacts with the legislative and appropriation committees. Those contacts took place only when new legislation was contemplated or at the time of processing a budget estimate. With many committees this took the form of perhaps only one, or at best, two such contacts in a year. In the long interval between meetings with the committees, there inevitably developed a gap of information as to progress and problems and also an accumulation of misunderstanding arising out of incidents or complaints which remained unresolved. It was our conclusion that the only way of meeting that problem was to seek for more frequent meetings in an atmosphere of informality. . . .

"We have been meeting with that committee [House Public Buildings and Grounds] on this basis for over two years and I think there is general agreement that the undertaking has been constructive. We meet ordinarily once a month and the occasion is one of informality and across-the-table discussion. There is no attempt to keep a record. On our part, we endeavor to report on the current housing scene as it has developed since the previous meeting, frankly identify problems, including failures as well as successes, and seek advice and reactions as to the progress of the program. . . .

"Generally, I think it has worked because it has provided both the committee and the agency an opportunity for discussion on the basis of the same set of facts. It has provided an occasion for the speedy resolving of complaints or misunderstandings and generally has de veloped an environment in which we have found a closer acquaintanceship and have built up a foundation of mutual respect and confidence. . . ."

In addition to the meetings, the National Housing Agency sent committee members a quarterly statement giving, in summary form, the current housing picture and a tentative look at the problems that needed attention in the months ahead.

On the other hand, the relations of the Office of Price Administration with Congress could hardly have been called amicable during most of that controversial agency's history. Involved here were the most difficult home-front problems of the entire war, and equally tough administration in the reconversion period. While he was head of the OPA, Chester Bowles fully realized the value of the procedure followed by the National Housing Agency. Unfortunately, the

OPA chief was able to have but one session with the House Banking and Currency Committee which supervised his agency. In June, 1945, speaking almost plaintively before the reorganization group, Mr. Bowles said:

> "All too frequently the only contact between agency heads and members of Congress occurs on critical issues which must be dealt with. As a result, the top men in the executive branches of the government often dread their contact with the legislators. Instead of a free-working relationship of intelligent people, all seeking the same general end, the contacts often are held in an atmosphere of suspicion, charges and misunderstanding.
>
> "A year ago I proposed to the Senate and House Banking and Currency Committees, which consider OPA legislation, a series of informal monthly meetings between the OPA executives and the members of the two committees. . . . In a sense, we would work with this parent committee or committees as administrative heads of a large business work with their board of directors.
>
> "I am confident that we in the OPA would benefit tremendously through such meetings. I personally would welcome a regular opportunity to go to a congressional group for advice and help in meeting the many difficult problems which we are called upon to solve.
>
> "I am equally confident that the members of the committees would develop, during the course of a year, a far clearer understanding of the huge administrative problems which we face in carrying out our responsibilities for controlling inflation and the equitable sharing of scarce commodities.
>
> "If this proposed plan was established as a general policy, each government bureau or department would have its own congressional group to which it would report regularly. With monthly meetings each group

would be kept fully informed on the attitude and points of view of the other."

Such proposed monthly meetings, with a personal report om the administrative chief or his liaison man at the Cap-l, should be incorporated into the schedules of all Senate d House committees with joint sessions held whenever ssible to save time and get information to all the persons rectly concerned.

The second point, day-to-day cooperation, involves hav-g liaison offices of the executive departments on Capitol ill. A few exist today, notably the Veterans Administration, vil Service Commission, Army, and Navy. It is a sound actice, but up to now has been poorly planned and very complete. Branch offices should be developed so as to pro-de continuous service to the committees and to individual embers; they could make a real contribution toward elim-ating irritations between the two ends of Pennsylvania venue.

We propose that quarters for liaison staffs for each federal partment and major agency be provided on Capitol Hill. he abolition of nearly seventy committees in the Reor-nization Act has freed much space which is now available r liaison offices. Each liaison office should be near the arters of the committee staff which will work closely with parent agency. It should be headed by a top official of the rticular executive unit with authority to speak for the oper Cabinet member or the agency director. It should be ffed adequately and provided with the best possible me-anical means of communicating with its downtown head-arters.

The liaison chief should transmit periodic reports to the mmittee on the progress of his department, and when

asked assist the committee chairman in arranging the agend
for monthly meetings and other more informal conferenc

There will always occur questions that need to be a
swered by an official high enough up in an agency to reco
nize their importance. A good example comes from the fil
of the old War Production Board. A member of Congre
was interested in a building program to make room for w
workers. Gas heating equipment was needed. He was to
at the WPB liaison office at the Capitol that there was r
chance of getting the equipment. However, the member
secretary was persistent and got the matter referred to tl
WPB office downtown, and the congressman took it up pe
sonally with the head of the branch. The application w
approved. Had the secretary not made the proper conta
downtown, the WPB might have been exposed to a slashir
attack for failing to act on a meritorious case. Here the tro
ble appears to have been with the inadequate liaison offic
We therefore recommend that liaison chiefs be of near-Ca
inet rank, perhaps an assistant secretary or a deputy admin
trator for congressional relations.

A third step that would end much bickering between tl
two ends of the Avenue and act as a practical curb on tl
occasional, admitted excesses of bureaucracy, is to devise
method for review of administrative orders and regulatior
Students and teachers of law recognize that the field of a
ministrative law has grown tremendously with the vast e
pansion of government. This has necessitated a wide deleg
tion of authority in many major pieces of legislation enact
in the past fifteen years. To carry out the laws passed I
Congress, agencies like the Securities and Exchange Cor
mission, the Civil Aeronautics Board, and the Federal Cor
munications Commission pass "laws" of their own in tl
form of regulations. The penalties for non-compliance

any cases are as severe in effect as the familiar fine and imprisonment schedules set out in the original laws passed by Congress.

Since it is necessary for the legislative branch to delegate such authority in the interest of achieving the goal for which the law was passed, there should be some kind of review to insure that administrative regulations conform to the intent of Congress. The rules of agencies should be tentative until the appropriate congressional committee has examined them. As soon as an agency has drafted regulations to effectuate a law of Congress, they should be presented to the proper House and Senate committees by the Capitol liaison officer of that agency, who would explain them and answer questions. Thereupon, these proposed regulations would be placed on the committee's docket and dated as to time of filing. If a majority of the full committee by formal vote did not object thereto within fifteen days from such filing, the rules and regulations would become effective. When Congress is in recess, review by mail should be arranged because so long a delay might seriously affect the enforcement of a given statute. In the La Follette-Monroney act, Congress requires that committees exercise "continuous watchfulness" over the agencies under their jurisdiction. This is a forward step but fails to provide adequate supervision machinery.

When proposed regulations are filed, the committee staff should include them in that day's report and prepare a digest in simple language for the members. The digest should then be printed in the *Congressional Record*. The *Federal Register* would continue to be used for the publication of the complete regulations.

We believe these suggestions go as far as possible in the desired direction of better executive-legislative teamwork without resorting to changes in the Constitution. We feel certain that lack of information is at the bottom of most real disputes between the two branches. The report an question period, the monthly meetings of agency chiefs ar committees of Congress, liaison staffs working daily at th Capitol, and systematic review of regulations will remed this lack of information and ensure better execution of law

CHAPTER 12

Curbing the Pressure Boys

L OBBYISTS! SAY THE WORD AND A FLOOD OF FACT AND FANCY
crowds through one's mind: Wall Street lining its pockets by
writing the tax laws . . . Main Street ground under the heels
of the pressure boys . . . Beautiful women and swank parties . . . Earnest men with placards and pamphlets . . . Millions spent freely to fix a tariff . . . Dimes collected la-
boriously to press a reform . . . Congress quaking before
the blasts of the Anti-Saloon League . . . Legislators taking
telephoned orders from agents of Big Business in hotel
suites . . . The power trust putting on the squeeze . . . The
suffragettes tugging at legislators' sleeves . . . Subtle bribery
. . . Bellowed threats . . . and so on and on, depending on
what one reads and who wrote it.

Volumes have been written about what is called the
"Third House of Congress," but this is a book concerned
only with the first two. We will state the problem, illustrate
various types of lobbying, and discuss remedial measures.
Our aim is to free Congress from the present *necessity* of
relying on lobbies of one kind or another in the great task
of writing laws for the nation.

Members of Congress, former members, and necessary employees are the only persons allowed inside the Senate and

House chambers. If one wishes to talk with a legislator, a page brings him the request, he leaves the floor and comes *outside* the chamber. In the Senate wing of the Capitol, such meetings take place in a beautifully appointed anteroom or *lobby*. On the House side, spacious corridors serve the same purpose.

Any day Congress is in session, one can see in these places little knots of people in earnest, sometimes heated discussion with various senators and congressmen. Some of the conversations represent lobbyists at work. Thus, acted out before one's own eyes, is a very simple form of the dictionary definition of lobbying: trying to get a bill through a legislative body by outside influence.

Any discussion of lobbies, because of existing evils in the system, is likely to be caustic. At the outset, therefore, we exempt from most of the criticism those good civic organizations that sometimes make skillful use of pressure tactics, but which work openly in the public interest in contrast to the backstage maneuvering of groups seeking only private gain. The good type of lobby, organized and run by unselfish civic leaders, frequently is of great help to members, especially to those interested in progressive legislation. We hesitate to single out any one of these praiseworthy organizations, but the League of Women Voters or the National Planning Association serve as excellent examples.

Many such civic-minded groups operate on a nationwide scale and put their collective strength behind a definite legislative program. The 1946-47 "platform" of the League calls for internationalization of atomic energy and its domestic development "in the public interest"; full United States acceptance of responsibility for strengthening the United Nations; government policies aimed at preventing inflation and deflation and achieving maximum production and employment; and finally, strengthening of the organization and procedures of Congress.

Groups such as the League are a constructive educational force in molding public opinion. They reach down into the local community to form study groups, hold debates, and stimulate discussion on national issues. They send skilled workers to Capitol Hill to prod members into action, and to argue with those who do not share their point of view. They are direct-action pressure groups. By the same token, they are a valuable factor in combating the natural inertia and habitual conservatism of regular political party organizations. They do not fit the traditional conception of a lobby. They are a healthy change from self-seeking pressure groups.

Lobbying has plagued Congress ever since speculators who had bought up sagging securities of the weaker states during the period of the Confederation (1781-1789), put through the First Congress a bill forcing these bonds to be redeemed at par. From that day to this, Washington has been infested with representatives of powerful interests who seek either to have laws passed that will mean more profits for their group, or to kill bills that would end some special privilege now enjoyed, often at the taxpayers' expense.

The confused and planless fashion which marks much of the business of drafting laws today makes Congress an easy prey for lobbies, although often an unsuspecting one. The power of these wholly unofficial but vital cogs in the legislative machinery continues to increase with the growth of government regulation of industry and commerce. Lobbies and pressure groups have become so powerful as to be called the "Invisible Government." This term is partly a misnomer. There is nothing invisible about the "legislative agents" and delegations that swarm the corridors of the Capitol and the office buildings in and out of session. They importune, cajole, and plead. They even threaten to defeat a member at the next election. There is nothing intangible about the messenger boys bearing armfuls of telegrams or the sacks of mail that arrive when a pressure group has whipped up a nationwide "Write or Wire Your Congressman" campaign.

Evidence of their effective work is always at hand. The clauses, amendments, and even entire bills conferring profitable privileges on a chosen few that slip through Congress, aren't legislative accidents. They are legislative miscarriages that encourage the belief that the national legislators are venal stooges of big business or spineless puppets of pressure groups. It would be a startling revelation to many if figures could be obtained showing the actual and proportionate number of important bills drafted originally in the office of some lawyer or trade association.

At the National Press Club or at other favorite meeting places of lobbyists around Washington, one hears such phrases as "our crowd got that bill through with almost no change," or "we did a good day's work yesterday when we knocked out that tax amendment," or "we have Senator X coming around okay." One wonders if members of Congress are complete suckers or just dumb. They are neither. They simply are so overburdened with work (the reorganization committee estimated it ran as high as eighty per cent "non-legislative") that lobby-inspired bills get by for want of adequate research aid and study time.

The situation is so bad that we make this serious charge: CONGRESS CANNOT FUNCTION TODAY WITHOUT LOBBYISTS. This damning indictment of the highest legislative body should arouse every thinking citizen to demand that drastic action be taken to make Congress self-reliant and truly representative of *all* the people.

To an increasing degree members of Congress rely on the executive departments and agencies to supply expert help, pertinent data, and competent witnesses. This is extremely useful, but also dangerous because shrewd bureaucrats can be as deviously persuasive as any special-interest representative. All too often, the only outside help available is none other than the lobbyist.

We do not suggest that members or committees should retreat into a congressional igloo, hibernate in solitude, spurn the advice and ideas of any person or group that may have something to contribute, and then emerge oracle-like, to strike off a law as if it were a commandment of Moses. We do contend that once evidence and suggestions, *made in open hearings,* are before any group of senators or congressmen, if legislation is necessary the committee should be able to prepare it without the aid of any lobbyist. When the school lunch bill was on the House floor in 1946, the committee in charge had to call in an outside specialist and hold an emergency executive session to unravel a snarl created by some amendments. In this case, the outsider happened to be a public-spirited woman skilled in the particular type of legislation; it could have been a special pleader.

There are several direct-action lobbies in Washington that exert a tremendous influence on national policies. The various veterans groups (American Legion, Veterans of Foreign Wars, and the new American Veterans Committee) have been the driving force behind the impressive array of bonus and pension legislation on the statute books. The soldier vote became potent following the War Between The States. This power was harnessed with the organization of the Grand Army of the Republic. General Philip Sheridan is credited with once saying to a GAR encampment that they "could drive an eight-horse team right through the United States Treasury."

Labor has been a highly explosive political factor for many

years; in the past decade its power has grown greatly. The Washington lobby of the Congress of Industrial Organizations is backed up by a national political organization extending all the way down to precinct captains. The CIO, the American Federation of Labor, and the railway brotherhoods, like the veterans organizations, have regular legislative agents at the Capitol to throw their weight around when votes are needed.

In this same general grouping are politically potent combinations of a quasi-public nature that unite the economic interests of certain regions of the country. Examples are the National Reclamation Association, which has the official sanction of the governments of a dozen Western states where irrigation is a live issue, the Inland Waterways Association, the Mississippi Valley Association, the Southern States Industrial Council, and others. Often big business groups interested in tariffs, taxes, subsidies, or opposing movements like TVA and the St. Lawrence Seaway, will lobby as intensively to capture control of these organizations as they do on Capitol Hill.

The peer of all direct-action lobbies was the omnipotent Anti-Saloon League which put over the Eighteenth Amendment. The man who cracked the whip for a decade on more than two-thirds of the Senate and House was the brilliant and indefatigable Wayne B. Wheeler, the League's legislative genius. Of him one of his biographers, Justin Stewart, states:

"He controlled six Congresses, dictated to two Presidents [Wilson and Harding], directed legislation in most of the states, picked the candidates for the more important elective and federal offices, held the balance of power in both Republican and Democratic parties, distributed more patronage than any dozen men, supervised

a federal bureau from outside without official authority
[the prohibition enforcement unit] and was recognized
by friend and foe alike as the most masterful and powerful single individual in the United States."

Wheeler, to the discomfort of some of his more idealistic
superiors in the League, wasn't too squeamish about the personal relationship of a legislator with John Barleycorn. His
only yardstick was that the man vote dry. A committeeman
might be dizzy with a hangover, but so long as he voted
with the Prohibitionists, he did not have to fear retribution
at the polls.

When a great issue of morality divides the nation as did
the Eighteenth Amendment, only a thoroughly reorganized
Congress can blunt the power that can be marshaled by both
sides. A skillful leader may muster an army of zealous workers fired with religious fervor, such as Wheeler had at his
disposal. For a time, he may be able to march a majority
of the entire nation to the polls. But a modernized Congress,
whose members are economically secure, can be a match for
a powerful lobbyist like Wheeler who could continue to call
the tune even after his cause was lost.

We turn now to more subtle forms of the art of lobbying;
first, to the "social lobby." Much has been written about the
social blandishments of Washington. There are plenty of
yarns about riotous living, "party girls," and bacchanalian
orgies. It is reported that the Ku Klux Klan once had an
effective agent who kept a fine yacht anchored in the Po-
tomac, and who on one occasion took aboard a cargo of congressmen and Follies girls. In his day this agent was called
"king of the lobbyists." However, such tales, and the occasional movies based upon them, are largely exaggerations.
Despite carelessly uttered charges of venality and bribe-tak-

ing, there are few cases either on record, or known to insiders, of members' actually accepting cash for legislative favors.

It is true that lobbyists do much entertaining in the national capital. The "cocktail circuit" is justly famous. Private dinners and parties are so numerous that night clubs and de luxe restaurants are far below the number that a visitor would expect in a world-famous capital. One interesting angle of the social lobby is the "visit our plant" technique. Members of Congress receive invitations to inspect a new factory or product, or see some new process demonstrated. It is all very educational. The host company arranges the Pullman reservations, has buses and cabs at the station, puts the party up at a beautiful hotel with excellent food. Wives are frequently included. The company pays all the expenses.

A spectacular example was the three-day "cruise" in 1940 from Newport News, Virginia, to New York City of the sumptuous liner *America*. Among the eight hundred passengers and the carload of whisky aboard was a solid trainload of members of Congress and newsmen from Washington. One could not help but be proud of the American enterprise and workmanship that had produced this great ship which during the war became the drab S.S. *West Point* and took American soldiers to world battlefields. The trip was excellent public relations for the shipping industry. The point to consider is that the shipping lines, or any other group that can indulge in such costly junkets, will usually be found at some future time pressing for congressional legislation—legislation which, while benefiting the industry involved, may not be in the best interest of the nation. Congress must be equipped to appraise all proposals objectively, regardless of what pleasant recollections they may have of the proponents.

Members of Congress do not shun the charms of the so-called social lobby. They enjoy gracious hospitality, and many useful ideas are gleaned from good talk at parties and dinners. They renew many acquaintances with constituents. (Of course, it is not always pure chance that one meets old friends from one's district on such occasions!) They get an opportunity to know fellow senators and congressmen better. Like many Washington radio and press correspondents, they get a lot of information. The power and excesses of the social lobby are overestimated. Nevertheless, it is a factor in determining attitudes toward problems up for congressional consideration.

Another feature of indirect lobbying is the individuals representing a single corporation or business who do remain largely "invisible" as far as the public is concerned, but who as a group make up an important part of the lobby picture. Such men gamble for high legislative stakes in terms of dollar rewards. Their pay, in some cases, is sheer loot. A member may be aware of their influence without even knowing who they are. Friends of a member often are the dupes of lobbyists who use them to convey a plausible argument for some apparently minor change in a pending measure. That "minor change" may turn out to be of great value to a particular manufacturer or contractor. An acquaintance once boasted indiscreetly that he could receive $10,000 for getting just two words, "cell blocks," into a Works Progress Administration authorization measure.

In 1913, James E. Watson, still one of Washington's best-known public figures, was charged with being a lobbyist for the National Association of Manufacturers. Watson had been a close friend of Speaker Joseph Cannon. The exposé claimed that Uncle Joe had given Jim an office right in the Capitol from where he could better conduct the "business" of the NAM. True or false, the accusation didn't deter Indiana voters later from sending Watson to the Senate; under

Hoover he became Majority Leader of the upper chamber.

The international effects of American tariff policies were not very much considered in the merry days when each session of Congress saw a horde of lobbyists use every trick in an extensive repertoire to get this or that rate hiked a little higher. The pressure boys went in the front doors and the back doors. The Hearst papers discovered that Charles L. Eyanson of the Manufacturers Association of Connecticut was sitting in Senator Hiram Bingham's office daily, helping write the Smoot-Hawley tariff bill. The sugar tariff battle in the 71st Congress saw financial and industrial giants move men like pawns. The domestic sugar interests (Louisiana cane growers and Western sugar beet combines) fought for a higher tariff against the importers (United Fruit, large chocolate candy manufacturers, and refiners) who wanted a low tariff. Both sides are reputed to have spent a million dollars each. Senator Reed Smoot of Utah was on the side of the domestic growers and he won. Frank H. Hitchcock, during his term as Postmaster General in the Taft administration, is credited with having gotten a boost in the copper tariff after using the office of the Senate Sergeant-at-Arms for his headquarters.

One common method of influencing an important vote is for a lobbyist to make a connection with an influential friend of the chairman of a committee considering a measure in which the pressure boy is interested. The backstage operator has the friend come to Washington, where he receives a thorough "indoctrination." Then he pays a visit to the committee chairman and "reasons" with his old friend. The unsuspecting legislator does not know that the lobbyist is waiting in a downtown hotel for a report from his stooge. And if this report proves unsatisfactory, the chairman's friend is equipped with fresh arguments and sent back to the Capitol.

There have been two devastating exposés of the worst phases of lobbying in recent years. The first was the exhaustive investigation conducted by Senator Thaddeus Caraway of Arkansas. The other was the famous public utility probe begun for Congress in 1928 by the Federal Trade Commission, which lasted several years and was one of the most thorough investigations ever made. In both cases thousands of pages of testimony were taken. The appalling power of private interests working for personal gain to pass the "right" kind of legislation was bared to the public.[1] Better federal regulation of the utilities developed from the latter inquiry.

The few main facts about these lobby investigations are quite simple. Highly paid propagandists posed as defenders of "States' rights," as spokesmen for the people "back home," as representative of "overwhelming" public opinion generally. Actually, these men were on the payrolls of individual corporations or were employed by closely organized trade associations. They were seeking to advance the financial interests of a group of private companies or a single industry at the expense of the nation. And at times they were so successful in hoodwinking the national legislators that some of the latter ceased to be representatives of the people.

One more insidious type of lobbying should be pointed out. In any system as large as the federal government, there are men and women who will seek to advance their own personal prestige, or to grab power merely for the sake of exercising more authority. They are a tiny minority of public servants, but they are the grasping bureaucrats who sometimes bring discredit upon the executive branch of the government. Within the departments, such aspiring executives are known as "builders." They look around for new

---

[1] See *Power Ethics*, by Jack Levin, New York, 1931.

functions and duties that will expand their units and increase their prestige—and pay. There are favors and services "beyond the line of duty" that such officials use in their lobbying on Capitol Hill. These come in very handily when the head of an agency seeks to keep control of funds or personnel that were approved in the previous year's budget, or which he secured in a special emergency appropriation. Among these favors is the power to allocate funds and projects to the states or districts of members of Congress who will play ball with them. Also, there is the ever-useful service of helping a member get somebody a job. Congress should be equipped to detect such schemers and keep them in their place. It should take *preventive* action, not demand expensive inquiries after damage has been done by administrative excesses.

The foregoing is a sketchy picture of the various types of lobbies at work. Their range and character is infinite; that word encompasses both the good and the bad. It embraces real forces for good in the body politic, such as the League of Women Voters and the small People's Lobby run by the highly respected Benjamin C. Marsh, whose activities are supported by contributions from liberals sharing his progressive views. It covers powerful economic groups such as the National Association of Manufacturers, the National Retail Druggists Association, which put over the so-called fair trade laws in all but two states after securing satisfactory legislation in the form of a rider attached to an appropriation bill, and the National Association of Real Estate Boards which combined with similar groups in this latter field to stage a terrific fight against the emergency housing program.

What is the remedy? Two famous Washington reporters, who have exposed many a lobbyist and his loot, are pessimistic. Writing in *More Merry-Go-Round,* Drew Pearson nd Robert S. Allen said dolefully: "Probably nothing ever vill be done." Two of their reasons are significant because he conditions they describe have become worse in the interval since their book was published. The first was the "slow and inefficient cumbersomeness of congressional machinery through which it is difficult to pass even the most innocuous bill without lobbying." Their second reason was the inefficiency of the average congressman and the fact that he is too busy or so slow that he must rely on outsiders to frame and explain legislative measures for him."

It is true that for one hundred forty-four years Congress made no attempt to deal with the problem directly. But Sentor Caraway did introduce a bill, following his lobby investigation, which would have required all persons seeking to influence legislation to register. Later, a small step was taken in this direction. The revelation of the activities of propaganda agents of foreign countries in the United States resulted in a law under which any person who engages in any type of public relations for another must register with the State Department. Most of these "agents" conduct harmless enterprises that seek to do a kind of chamber of commerce job for their respective foreign employers.

The reorganization committee recognized the difficulty when it said that "the problem of safeguarding free expression of the will of the people from distortion is a difficult one. Rather than stifle any such expression, your committee hesitates to make any recommendation upon the control of lobbyists or pressure groups." However, the report did urge legislation similar to the Caraway plan for registration of "organized groups and their agents" and requiring quarterly statements of their legislative expenditures. The La Follette-Monroney act of 1946 put these recommendations into effect.

We heartily approve this action. It will be valuable in

identifying witnesses at committee hearings who make varying claims as to whom and what they represent. However, such a step will hardly disturb the invisible government that shuns the open light of a committee hearing as it would a plague—the men who sit unobtrusively in the galleries and watch subtly laid plans mature in innocent-sounding amendments that mean money in their pockets, the men who "work both sides of the street" with campaign contributions, and are skilled in applying indirect pressure that causes many an honest member of Congress to wince.

Furthermore, some of the smart pressure boys already think they have figured a way around the new registration requirement. Many of the lawyer-lobbyists can prove to any court that they do not devote a "major portion" of their time to influencing legislation. For example, a tax specialist with the right connections may need only a few weeks out of an entire year to safeguard the interests of his client in any tax legislation that might be considered.

Also, many trade associations can demonstrate that the greater portion of their time and money is spent in form of "service" such as gathering statistics, working with the departments, representing members before various agencies, arranging district meetings and national conventions, and so on. Some of these groups plan to designate only one employee or official as "legislative agent" and report only his salary and expenses. Thus, when an association gives a big cocktail party or dinner at which government officials may far outnumber the members of Congress invited, the expenditure is not likely to be reported.

The 1946 reorganization law made an excellent start on the lobby problem. However, the tentacles of the invisible government reach into every phase of lawmaking. The most complete remedy to curb, perhaps even destroy the admitted power of the pressure boys, is to push through a complete modernizing and streamlining of the national legislature, including the important changes we have recommended in procedure on the floor of the House and Senate and the suggestions for better liaison between the executive and legislative branches. Not until then will there be an answer to the dour predictions of Pearson and Allen. If Congress will finish the job so well begun—in addition to the registration measure—we can expect three results that will curb the lobbyist.

The first derives from the restoration of the true deliberative function of Congress in all phases, from procedure on the floor, in committee, down to the individual member. The elimination of useless committees, the installation of electric voting, destruction of the facility for filibuster, the reduction of irritants between the executive and legislative branches, and better executive liaison on Capitol Hill—all this, together with the adoption of practical methods for relieving members of the intolerable burden of non-legislative work, will release precious hours for study and research. It will mean more time to read bills and committee reports on recommended legislation, time to hear that last witness who may put his finger on a hitherto unnoticed weakness in a pending measure, time to force explanations on the floor of sudden amendments. When Congress has time to do these things, a mighty blow will have been struck at the backstage manipulators. If such reforms had prevailed in 1944—to cite but one example—we do not believe that the House would have approved, as it did by a 283-54 vote, a lobbyist's bill to nullify a Supreme Court decision which held that insurance companies are engaged in interstate business and thus subject to the anti-trust laws.

The second result will be to restore to Congress the ability to draft bills, evaluate "expert" testimony, and assemble its own statistics on the possible effects of proposed legislation *on the nation as a whole*. Hitherto, this function has rested too largely with the lawyer-lobbyist, the pressure groups, and the legislative experts attached to the executive departments.

Strengthening of the bill-drafting service in the two houses, enlargement of the Legislative Reference Service of the Library of Congress, and above all, the adequate staffing of committees with expert personnel, and individual offices with more competent help, are all steps toward this goal. Few people today realize how often Congress has been forced to rely on persons who have no official connection with the government when drafting and perfecting legislation. Committees, with hit-or-miss staffs, have been totally unprepared to deal with this evil. The overambitious departmental bureaucrat is not the answer. Even the House Appropriations Committee, the best-organized unit in Congress, can be deceived. A bureau employee, upon being promoted to chief clerk, approached his first budget hearings with some trepidation. His remarks must remain anonymous:

"I had heard weird tales of the inquisition I would face. I had been told these congressmen knew more about our work than we did ourselves. Imagine my surprise when members of this subcommittee asked only routine and often aimless questions. They did not display any great knowledge of our work. Why, if we had been so disposed, we could have gotten away with murder with that bunch."

Is any better illustration needed?

The third and perhaps the most effective of all measures to curb the unscrupulous lobbyist is to raise congressional salaries and adopt an equitable retirement system for members. We speak carefully here; it is our honest conviction that the people do not often elect crooks to Congress. But there are some men grown poor in Congress who find it impossible to make ends meet and therefore, unconsciously or otherwise, hesitate to alienate groups whose support, financial and ballot-wise, they may need at the next election.

Consider the predicament of any member now in his late fifties or sixties who has given long and satisfactory service, and who has broken all business ties many years ago in order to remain in Congress. His age makes it difficult for him to reenter a business or profession. He has not been able to save enough for any appreciable income. It is only natural that such a man be tempted to take the popular course, or lend an ear to a persuasive voice when highly controversial bills are up for a vote. He's got to keep on being reelected to have a job.

The better pay and the retirement plan provided for in the La Follette-Monroney act, will give senators and congressmen more independence of thought and action generally, and will dissipate the temptations and sometimes implied obligations that go with campaign contributions. In our opinion, the salary rise and pension system set up in the 1946 Reorganization Act will be even more effective in restraining the pressure boys than the lobby registration feature. Both steps have been long overdue.

Congress has beaten its breast over the surrender of some of its power to the Executive. Equally dangerous has been its abdication of power to the lobbyists. The latter's techniques are up to date. They use every modern means to exploit the opportunities afforded them by the present inefficient organization of Congress. The most effective way that the national legislature can curb the pressure boys is to do its business more efficiently than they do theirs.

CHAPTER 13

Letters That Really Count

THE THIRD ARTICLE IN THE FAMOUS BILL OF RIGHTS SAYS:
"Congress shall make no law . . . abridging . . . the right
of the people . . . to petition the Government for a redress
of grievances." Thus did the Founding Fathers recognize
the fundamental right of the citizen to express his opinion
to Congress, and protect in the Constitution the privilege of
writing to one's senator or congressman.

That is how congressional mail started. This Capitol Hill
mail has now reached the stupendous average volume of
more than 100,000 pieces daily. More than eighty employees
are required to man the Capitol post offices in normal periods. When floods of mail result from controversies such as
that over "packing" the Supreme Court, the fight to regulate
utilities, and, more recently, the battles over the OPA and
regulation of labor unions, the normal figure often doubles.
In fact, it seems almost odd today that a constitutional
amendment once was thought necessary to protect the citizens. No member of Congress would remain in office beyond
the next election if he disregarded the petitions and letters
he gets from constituents.

When the author first came to Washington from Tennessee in 1939, he followed the pleasant custom of paying his
respects to the Speaker of the House, who at that time was
Representative Will Bankhead of Alabama. During the
course of conversation this question was asked: "What is the

secret of long tenure? How do members get reelected term after term without substantial opposition?"

Speaker Bankhead replied without hesitation: "It is a simple one. Give close and prompt attention to your mail. Your votes and speeches may make you well known and give you a reputation, but it's the way you handle your mail that determines your reelection." In the intervening years the solid truth of his answer has become evident. Members who desire to make Congress their career follow the advice given by Speaker Bankhead.

Senator Kenneth McKellar of Tennessee, a veteran of more than thirty-two years in Congress, has a rigid office rule that requires every communication received to be answered on the same day. It may be a simple form letter that says the matter referred to is being investigated and that further information will follow, but the constituent is impressed. Senator McKellar credits to this practice much of the success of his long career at the Capitol.

Mail is the most practicable way of maintaining a close relationship between Congress and the people. In the past few years when sessions have been almost continuous, members have had little time to visit their home states and districts. When they can get away from Washington, their time is consumed largely by people with specific and usually personal problems. There is little opportunity to take soundings on reaction to legislation that may be pending. In the author's particular district not more than one in a thousand constituents visits the office in any single year. Hence, the chief reliance in "feeling the pulse of the people" must be placed on mail.

In the early days of the Republic, mail, of course, was scant. It did not become a great physical burden until recently. Until the turn of this century, national legislation touched the daily lives of Americans only briefly, if at all, except in time of war. As late as the 1920's, President Calvin

Coolidge said the federal government could cease to operate and the average citizen wouldn't know the difference for three months.

All that is changed today. With the great strides in education, the wide dissemination of news by radio, daily newspapers, and magazines, and the growth of huge organizations whose programs are affected by the federal government, has come a vast expansion in government itself. Add to these facts the modern facilities for personal communication such as the typewriter, telephone, mimeograph, improved telegraph, and speedier printing, and one has the answer to those millions of letters that arrive annually at the Capitol.

A predecessor from the Third Tennessee District, Representative John A. Moon, had a single secretary who penned replies on the bottom or back of the letter sent in by the constituent. Former Senator Burton K. Wheeler of Montana can recall when 20 letters in one day was "big" mail. A survey of several congressional offices indicates that the average member now receives more than 100 communications daily. Of course, it runs unevenly. The more controversial bills a member sponsors, the more mail he gets. The size and type of district naturally affects the volume too. A Western senator, the storm center of one great debate, received as many as 7000 letters in a single day. Most members now have three secretaries devoting the greater part of their time to the bundles of mail delivered to each office four times a day.

The public should understand how this mail is evaluated, how it is handled, and how much of it really influences legislation. Which are the letters that really count?

Thousands of letters arrive every day asking personal favors and assistance with no direct bearing on the legislative duties of the members. This might be called "constituent service" mail. Its range is infinite. A citizen doesn't know the head of the Veterans Administration, or the Secretary of the Treasury, and he has business with their departments. So he writes his senator or congressman. Some requests are ludicrous. Former Representative Joe Byrns, Jr., of Tennessee tells of a letter asking him to go to the Patent Office and ascertain what hadn't been patented so the writer could make a patent application therefor. Constituent service isn't confined to mail. They come in person. Visitors are seldom interested in legislation, but they take time from legislative work.

Then there is a good run of requests for information about pending bills, for copies of hearings or reports, for explanations of amendments or of a rule proposed by a bureau. They are answered carefully and promptly, and form a part of the index to public interest in given issues.

Now come the petitions, chain telegrams, form letters, postcards, pamphlets, brochures, and individual letters, all aimed directly at influencing votes. This is the "pressure mail." Let us consider petitions first. They have been used longer and have an official status. They vary from a dozen names on a single postcard to huge rolls measured in hundreds of yards and delivered to the Capitol by truck.

Petitions may come from patrons on a small rural mail route, or they may be lists containing thousands of signatures gathered in every state in the union by a national organization. In the House those for or against a pending bill are "dropped in the hopper." This is a small wooden box attached to the side of the Clerk's desk on the House floor. The same receptacle is used for filing bills. The next day the *Congressional Record* carries under a regular subhead, "Petitions, Etc.," insertions like this:

"Under Clause 1 of Rule XXII of the House, petitions and papers were laid on the Clerk's desk, and referred as follows:

"581 by Mr. Mahon: Petition of about 175 farmers and business men of Scurry County, Texas; urging parity prices for farm commodities, etc.; to the Committee on Agriculture."

Petitions, memorials, and resolutions go to the committees having jurisdiction of the subject matter and normally they are never heard of again. No one reads them. They gather dust in Capitol files until finally carried away. They seldom influence legislation.

Legislators know it is possible to get many people to sign a petition for almost any cause, worthy or otherwise. Some time ago in Knoxville, Tennessee, booths were placed on the main street. Bells were rung to attract the attention of passersby. In this manner thousands of names were secured on a petition asking presidential aid for Earl McFarland, an escaped convict from the Washington, D.C., jail who was under death sentence.

The author once received a petition signed by 170 patrons of the post office at Daylight, Tennessee, protesting the proposed removal of that office to another location three miles distant. The signatures were obtained by a businessman whose store was near the old site. A few weeks later there arrived another petition signed by a number of constituents saying the new location would be in the public interest. *Many patrons signed both lists!*

In 1945 a House judiciary subcommittee headed by Representative Sam Hobbs of Alabama was holding hearings on the Bryson bill to outlaw the sale of intoxicating beverages near Army camps. Petitions asking favorable action began arriving by the ton. One side of Judge Hobbs's spacious reception room was piled ceiling high with these documents.

Representative Emanuel Celler of New York and others opposing the measure became alarmed at the weight of the "pros" and told the opposition to get busy. In a short time truckloads of petitions against the bill were received. And so it goes, but regardless of length or weight, petitions are of little value as a persuasive force.

Equally ineffective are the chain telegrams. Dozens are received each week. Individuals, corporations, and organizations seem to think they are the best way to impress a member with the urgency of a cause. Actually, many such telegrams have the opposite effect. Unless the message is in fact urgent, a letter may be more useful. It is easy for an executive, well supplied with secretaries and finances, to dictate a telegram to one member and direct that the same wire be sent to the entire congressional delegation from his state, or even to every member of Congress.

Some groups drumming up pressure collect the cost of a chain telegram from their members at a meeting and get permission to send it over their names. This is a popular pressure tactic but largely ineffectual. When the same telegram is sent to several congressmen, the text is run off on a duplicating machine and the individual names of members inserted. The senators and congressmen know they are being circularized. When a large number of telegrams on the same subject is received, they usually get the treatment they merit—a mimeographed acknowledgment.

Here are some typical chain telegrams:

CONGRESSMAN ESTES KEFAUVER HOUSE OFFICE BLDG WASHDC. THE JOHN DOE LEAGUE REPRESENTS THOUSANDS OF INVESTORS THROUGHOUT THE COUNTRY. WE STRONGLY ENDORSE HR 6259 AND URGE THAT THIS ANTI-ROYALTY MEASURE BE REPORTED FAVORABLY.

JOHN DOE LEAGUE INC.

HON ESTES KEFAUVER HOUSE OFFICE BLDG WASHDC PER-
SONAL SUBJECT EXTENSIONS OF SELECTIVE SERVICE.
YOU KNOW THAT THE EYES OF THE OVERWHELMING MA-
JORITY OF PARENTS AND SONS OF THIS NATION ARE
FOCUSED UPON YOU WITH THE EARNEST HOPE THAT YOU
WILL GIVE BACK TO THE KIDS OF THE NATION THEIR
INHERENT RIGHTS AND FREEDOMS. MAY I PROPOSE THE
FOLLOWING AMENDMENTS. DRAFT AGE TO BE 20 OR 21.
ALL SCIENTIFIC STUDENTS IN COLLEGES OR UNIVERSI-
TIES SHOULD BE EXEMPTED. DRAFT SHOULD BE SUS-
PENDED MAY 15TH TO DETERMINE WHETHER WITH IN-
CREASED SALARIES VOLUNTARY ENLISTMENTS WILL PRO-
VIDE NECESSARY REPLACEMENTS.   RESPECTFULLY
YOURS.

JOHN DOE

While the author does not question for a moment the
privilege of such petitioners, he does advise them that the
chain wire is not going to have much effect on his vote.

The next items in the pressure-tactic catalogue are form
letters and chain postcards. Organizations sometimes send
their members cards which are to be signed and forwarded
to Washington. They arrive in batches, as many as a hundred at a time, and when this occurs it is obvious that someone is pumping the pressure bellows. Frequently, of course,
the pumping is done for a worthy cause or a piece of constructive legislation. Here are four samples picked at ran-
dom, with the spaces for signature left blank:

Hon. Estes Kefauver,
House of Representatives,
Washington, D.C.
Sir:

There is now pending a bill for mobile libraries, introduced by Senator Lister Hill and
Representative Emily Taft Douglas, and this
letter conveys to you our earnest desire that

you support this worthy measure. In our State
it is estimated that more than one million persons would profit from this bookmobile service.
During the war traveling libraries were successfully used for the armed forces stationed in
inaccessible localities.

In rural areas, those now without library
facilities in schools and in the home would, for
four years at least, be enabled to have book
culture, if there is a yearly federal grant of
$25,000 to each state. Individual states would
provide up to a maximum of $50,000 annually.

In Tennessee 40% of the population has no
access to library facilities. Over the nation,
35,000,000 adults and school age boys and girls
are denied the blessing of books. We pray that
you do your utmost in behalf of these under-
privileged people.

                              Respectfully,
                              Club Name ....
                                       ....
                                            Secretary
Number of members......

                                   May 20, 1946.
Honorable Sir:

        Beer, the beverage of moderation, is the drink of the working
man.
        Why this curtailment?
        No wheat is used in its production.
        Thousands of brewery workers are idle.   Thousands of retail-
ers and wholesalers are needlessly affected.
        Labor connected with distribution of beer is idle.
        Business investments of huge amounts are endangered.
        Our State and Federal Treasuries will show a loss of millions
of dollars.
        Again, why this curtailment?

Name_____ Address_____

City_____State_____

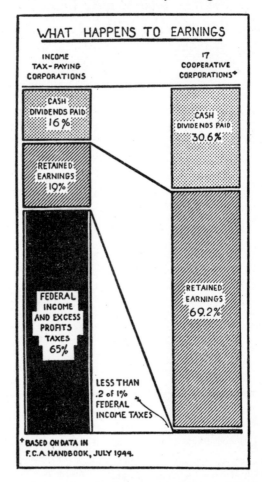

Why does the Government allow the condition pictured above to continue? It results in—

(1) Loss of tax revenue to which the Government is entitled.

(2) Use by co-operatives of money which they should pay in taxes to build vertical trusts which threaten the existence of taxpaying small businesses.

Name..

Address...

Dear Congressman:

      Stockings are important to health as well as appearance. I need hosiery desperately and our stores have none.

      Won't you help?

      Please urge the Civilian Production Administration to allocate rayon yarns to hosiery mills until nylon stockings are available in adequate quantities.

      Thank you for your interest and attention.

      Name_____

      Address_____

The letter concerning stockings arrived along with 260 others. All were addressed to "Estes T. Kefauver, M.C." The author's middle initial *not* being "T," this was a dead giveaway of the common origin of the pressure. The drumbeater had been grossly careless in not even checking the name of the man whose assistance was solicited.

The masterminds behind these mass-production mail campaigns devote much time and skill to composing such congressional form letters. They use the latest duplicating devices in attempts to make the letters look like individually written communications. With some excellent multigraph work one has to look twice before realizing it is a form epistle.

The form letter strategy is varied. Members of Congress frequently receive a number of letters on a particular subject. The language is different in each, but all convey substantially the same message and make the same request. In May of 1946 the author received sixty letters in one week from industrial firms. The thought expressed by all was the necessity for balancing the federal budget and reducing bureau expenditures. They were well written and began to look impressive.

However, one member of this particular industry was apparently short of secretarial assistance. He just sent on the bulletin from his trade organization and asked that it be given consideration. The bulletin gave the organization members instructions, suggesting that each write his congressman to urge reduction in federal spending, express alarm at the rising national debt, and demand that government costs be reduced. The bulletin was careful to advise each member to write in his own language and *not to mention that his letter had been suggested by the association.*

Tactics of this nature do not rate very high in influencing a member of Congress.

Finally, comes the pamphlet—in many forms. It may be a hurried job run off in fine type on cheap paper, or it may be an expensively printed brochure in attractive colors and well illustrated with charts and pictures. Many of these are valuable for reference, but should be digested and used only with care to keep in mind the special interest of the person or group that spent the money to prepare and distribute them.

Senators and congressmen aren't often fooled by these various types of pressure mail. They do not judge the sentiment of their constituency entirely by the preponderance of inspired letters or telegrams. Some time ago, former Representative Clare Luce of Connecticut remarked that she had received twenty pounds of mail against a pending proposal and twenty-four pounds for it. She added quickly that the poundage did not necessarily determine the sentiment of her district or the validity of the pro and con arguments. In short, letters that count aren't measured on a postage scale.

It would, however, be inaccurate to say that petitions, form letters, chain telegrams, and other forms of mass propa-

anda are discounted entirely. Pressure mail forces a member
to find out what the legislation is about, to give it some
study, and to inform himself on both sides of the issue. And
by study of the forces behind a pressure campaign, he may
get considerable light on the real purposes of the legislation. We do not imply that all propaganda tactics are used
for selfish interests. However, an alert member will do his
own investigating.

Petitions and mass letters sometimes have another value.
If a member has decided to vote a certain way on a bill, or
to recommend a certain person for a postmaster job, a bundle
of communications favoring his decisions can be used effectively to buttress the position he has taken, or to defend
himself against protests of angry constituents. On one occasion the author recommended the appointment of a rural
carrier. It proved to be an unpopular selection. However, in
the office was a petition signed by practically every patron on
the mail route involved. Several who protested the recommendation had signed this petition. Faced with this fact,
they made excuses, but could not complain too bitterly of
the choice that had been made.

When one's vote on a national issue is challenged, it is
somewhat comforting to be able to tell disgruntled constituents that "I had twenty letters sustaining my vote to every
one I received against it." By and large, however, members
know that pressure groups often produce such extreme dis-
proportions through an outpouring that may represent only
a relatively small minority of the people in a state or district. Members usually know their people, their prejudices,
virtues, and weaknesses, and how certain groups among their
constituencies react to various philosophies of government.
When they lose this knowledge, they usually become ex-
members.

What, then, are the letters that really count? To over simplify a moment, they are those from people who count. They come from people who are known to the member as taking a national viewpoint. He has friends who are interested in his record and his future. Letters from these friends are valued. Messages from students of government and economics are helpful. For example, Dr. Frank Prescott, head of Chattanooga University's School of Government, writes the author frequently and at length. His knowledge is respected and his opinion valued.

A member of Congress usually has several key men and women in each county of his constituency. When he needs information about applicants for a job or the effect of some legislation on that county or area, he writes to them and their replies count. Frequently these people will be asked to give their opinion of the public reaction in their respective communities to national issues being debated in Congress. They "feel out" the sentiment and advise the member. Letters from schoolchildren often have a freshness and display original thinking that is valuable.

Congressmen want details and not generalities. Letters from an individual which give the facts of how a particular proposal would affect him as an individual, a farmer, a worker, or a businessman, always are welcomed. A candy concern that simply protests generally against reducing the sugar quota doesn't make much impression. If that firm advises that the reduction will decrease its operation by forty per cent and cause one hundred twenty people to lose their jobs, then sugar legislation is going to get special attention.

Two congressmen stressed this point in discussing effective mail. Former Representative George Outland of California, writing in *The Reader's Digest,* said: "When possible, make your letter apply to the local situation. Tell your Representative how a national issue affects your community, your busiless or your family. Be specific, frank, factual, natural." Representative Brooks Hays of Arkansas in the *Congressional Record* suggests that, to be effective, letters should "give reasons for your position. You may have some ideas about the application of measures to local and particular situations that have not occurred to others." One penciled page from a respected farmer or businessman in this category will outweigh in influence a hundred form letters inspired by a pressure drive.

Expressions from individuals and groups that have studied a problem are most helpful. Organizations such as the League of Women Voters, the American Association of University Women, the Federation of Women's Clubs, the National Planning Association, and the American Bar Association devote much time to analyzing measures before Congress. They have no special axes to grind and their well-reasoned communications are always beneficial.

Another type of letter that counts heavily is somewhat hard to define. Its outstanding feature is its utter sincerity. A rural citizen may write in crude hand on a sheet of school tablet paper or even on brown wrapping stock. One can see that the writer has erased one word to substitute another. The congressman knows that this citizen has pondered the subject matter for a long time and that he means what he writes.

A word about the letters that don't come. Anyone with a personal or selfish interest in a proposal will write freely and get as many others as possible to support him, and where possible enlist the aid of political leaders. The new member of Congress may think these communications reflect public opinion in his bailiwick. Actually, it may be just the opposite. The average citizen who does not have any peculiar interest in a measure is not apt to be vocal. The people who do not write expect their senator or congressman to "do the right thing," and it doesn't occur to them to lend a helping hand with an encouraging letter.

At one point in the 1946 OPA fight, congressional mail was running eighty per cent *against* OPA extension, yet a Gallup poll showed the public was more than seventy per cent *in favor of* extension. Proposals for extension of Selective Service brought a ten to one ratio of opposition mail, yet all polls showed a majority of the people felt that the draft should be continued.

It is not unusual to hear a congressman in Washington say something like this: "I've got to get out of town for a few days. When I sit in my office and read complaints, criticism, and threats, day after day, and get no encouragement, I begin to think the country is going to the dogs." It is true that ninety per cent of the mail asks for something or predicts extinction at the polls if a member does not do so and so. The rare letter of appreciation is like a rainbow in a storm-clouded sky. The average legislator is trying to do his best, and a little written encouragement gives his morale a terrific boost. When that happens, he is a more useful member of Congress.

The purpose of this book is to show how Congress can do its work more effectively and how its members can do a better, more efficient job. More "letters that really count" will be a real public contribution toward achieving that goal. And letters that tell members to complete the job of congressional reorganization will contribute to the effective government which this age demands.

CHAPTER 14

"M.C." or "W.R." — Can One Be Both?

MANY CRITICS OF THE NATIONAL LEGISLATURE CLAIM THAT the principal function of a member of Congress, particularly on the House side, is to be a glorified errand boy for enough people in his district who swing enough votes every two years to keep him in office. What this criticism fails to recognize is that senators and representatives today hold two distinct and different jobs. Both are important and the voters expect the men and women they send to Washington to do both well. Under present conditions, that is practically impossible. Fortunately, remedies for this situation are at hand.

The first, most important, and too often neglected of these two jobs is symbolized by the "M.C." on congressmen's cards that admit visitors to the galleries of the legislative chambers. There one sees (sometimes, at least) what the "M.C." stands for: Member of Congress, making the laws for the nation. That is what the Constitution says he was elected to do.

That duty implies that members have time to concentrate on the difficult task of writing good laws to meet national problems. It assumes that they will provide themselves with the best brains and most useful means of research to make a continuous study of national needs. As individuals, and as a group, that duty means they must provide intelligent leadership for American citizens in preserving a proper balance between the national and international interests of the nation on the one hand, and state, regional, and local interests on the other.

The Constitution also places no restriction on a member's being reelected. That is how the second job probably developed. When a constituent asks his senator or representative to get him a room in a crowded Washington hotel, and he receives a reply from the member's office, the letters "M.C." in the upper right-hand corner of the franked envelope would be more accurate if they were "W.R."; "Washington Representative." Doubtless some members overdo the personal favor and errand business. However, as government grows, this phase of their work—being the Washington representative for constituents—becomes more important.

The La Follette-Monroney committee recognized this new development, and sought to relieve members of the great burden of non-legislative work. One of its major recommendations was that each senator and representative be authorized to "employ a high-caliber administrative assistant at an annual salary of $8,000 to assume non-legislative duties now interfering with the proper study and consideration of national legislation."

Members had testified before the committee that "Washington Representative" work was consuming as high as eighty per cent of their time. This should have convinced Congress of the importance of relieving members of an intolerable burden. The committee could have presented a stronger case if it had drawn attention to the amount of time and money that *private* or *special* interests allot to their Washington activities. In the act that finally passed, only the Senate provided for administrative assistants, while the House did nothing beyond allotting assistants to the Speaker and the Majority and Minority Leaders.

The business of being the Washington representative for a private concern or for some organization, public or private, is a fast-growing and often lucrative line of work in the nation's capital. The number of these special representatives increases constantly, and many former members of Congress are among them. Some have large staffs to handle liaison work with Congress, with the vast labyrinth of government departments and agencies, and with other special groups which make Washington their national headquarters. One addition to these representatives' ranks in 1945 that made news came when the Motion Picture Producers and Distributors of America named Eric Johnston, president of the Chamber of Commerce of the U.S., as their top Washington man at a reputed $100,000-a-year salary, and bought one of the most expensive pieces of property in the capital on which to erect an elegant headquarters building.

Annual budgets of from $25,000 to $75,000 for private Washington representatives are not uncommon. In most cases, the pay is earned because the job requires a specialized knowledge, ability to influence people, an office capable of getting information from the proper source quickly, of answering thousands of inquiries, and an insight into the trends and temperaments of Washington officialdom. Not every such Washington representative is a lobbyist, but all lobbyists are in this category, although they have different titles. They may simply have "Law Office" on the door, or even work anonymously from a hotel suite.

Each of these men and women represents a special interest or group. It may be a very important billion-dollar corporation, or a great service organization such as the veterans groups. It may be an historical-patriotic society like the

Daughters of the American Revolution, or an education segment like the Association of American Universities, or even a great religious organization like the National Catholic Welfare Conference. Both labor and management have their Washington ramparts well manned, as evidenced by the elaborate headquarters of the American Federation of Labor, the United States Chamber of Commerce, the American Retail Federation, and the Congress of Industrial Organizations.

Some W.R.'s will claim that they speak for a thousand stockholders in a company; or for tens of thousands of housewives or mothers; or for hundreds of thousands of businessmen; or even for millions of union members. This one fact applies to all of them: *they represent some special interest, or some special segment of the public.*

Who represents all of the people? The obvious answer is: Congress. And constituents more and more are demanding that individual senators and congressmen give them just about the same kind of service for which the special groups hire private Washington representatives—a new workload entirely over and above the traditional statutory functions of a member of Congress.

In the Constitution a citizen cannot find any language that requires a member to take him to the Reconstruction Finance Corporation to meet officials who can help him with a government loan, or to some other bureau where he needs a personal contact. There's nothing in that document or in any rules of the Senate or House which obligates a member to help someone's Aunt Minnie get a job with the Veterans Administration, or to arrange a sightseeing trip when Grandmother visits Washington. But in nine cases out of ten, a senator or representative must do these things if he is to stay in office.

New millions learn to read and write every year and, so

it would seem, test their new-found ability by inditing "Dear Congressman, Will you——?" The telegraph and typewriter have made it that much easier for the American citizen to dash off a request asking Senator X to do some favor; thousands of longhand letters continue to arrive. The automobile and a splendid highway system have made it easy to come to Washington personally, and it's a sure bet the visitor will look up his congressman. If a member isn't available to each and all, the opposition candidate in the next election picks up some votes. There seems to be something about the radio, too, that accounts for tens of thousands of letters that must be answered. One gets the impression that listeners sit with pen in hand just hoping some speech or newscast will give them an excuse to write to Washington.

We do not condemn the practice of letter-writing. Discounting the highly organized pressure campaigns by minorities, it is one of the healthier signs in the national life today. But it does add uncounted man-hours of work to the office of each senator and congressman. Former Secretary of State James F. Byrnes, who sat in both the Senate and the House, writing in the *American Magazine* described this new characteristic of service on Capitol Hill:

> "The people of a congressional district have come to look upon a Congressman, not as their representative in Congress, but as their representative in Washington. The average man who has business with a department of a state government seldom thinks of communicating with the state legislators. But if he has business with the executive departments of the Federal Government, he calls upon the Senator or the Congressman to attend to his business with the Government."

There is no better way to demonstrate the accuracy of Mr. Byrnes's observations than to make a list of all the things a congressman may do on a typical day. Many excellent compilations of this type have been published, some giving a minute-by-minute account. The author didn't make any such detailed record (there wasn't the time!) but one night during the 79th Session jotted down some notes on what had been done that day. With apologies to Mrs. Eleanor Roosevelt, here is the author's own "My Day." Each item is classified as to whether it falls in the traditional "Member of Congress" category, or should be credited to the new and growing job of "Washington Representative." All references to "district" refer to the Third Tennessee Congressional District which the author represents.

1. Up at 7 A.M., breakfasted with family while scanning morning paper headlines. Opened the mail delivery which reaches the apartment before time to leave for the office. Finished reading local morning papers while my wife drove me to the new House Office Building. (*M.C.* and *W.R.* Any batch of mail brings requests from constituents for some kind of personal service. Reading the daily papers is part of an M.C.'s duty to keep himself posted on what is happening here and abroad.)

2. Arrived at the office at 8:45 A.M., the usual time. Staff already had opened some fifty letters which came in the first deliveries, and arranged them for inspection. For next hour, dictated replies to those requiring policy or personal answers, and indicated how other mail was to be handled. Glanced through several pamphlets such as come in every mail. One was a study of building costs issued by the National Housing Administrator, Wilson Wyatt, and was put aside in the hope that it could be read before the housing bill came up for debate. (*M.C.* and *W.R.* Some of the correspondence concerned work to be done with the executive depart-

ment, and some related directly to pending or proposed legislation.)

3. Discussed with the Rural Electrification Administration the problem of securing a loan for a cooperative in the district. (*M.C.*)

4. Talked with the dean of local university to get a constituent's son into this crowded institution. (*W.R.*)

5. Went with a manufacturer from the district to the War Assets Administration to discuss the possibilities of his buying a building that had been declared surplus. (*W.R.*)

6. Called on the chief architect of the Veterans Administration with an architect from the district who wanted a job on the new veterans facility that is going to be built in Chattanooga, chief city in my district. (*W.R.*)

7. Gave interviews to four newsmen on a bill to amend the Clayton anti-trust act that I was sponsoring. Two of the reporters came to the office and the other two got their stories over the telephone. (*M.C.*)

8. Long distance call from Cleveland, Tennessee, from a friend (and constituent) who asked me to get hotel reservations for several persons arriving the next week. (*W.R.*)

9. Called Surgeon General's office to see if it were possible to secure waiver of physical disability for an appointee to West Point. Father, who is constituent, very anxious to have son enter the Academy. (*M.C.* Not strictly a legislative duty, but appointments to the military and naval academies long have been a congressional prerogative.)

10. Interviewed a friend desiring to be admitted to practice before the Supreme Court of the United States, and wrote him a letter of endorsement. (*Personal.*)

11. Arrived late at a Judiciary Committee meeting (I am a member), but did not remain until end of session

because of engagements to meet some constituents back in the office. (*M.C.* and *W.R.*)

12. Called Postmaster General's office to recommend favorable action on extension of a rural route in district. (Borderline but listed as *M.C.* because it was service to the district rather than to an individual.)

13. Lunched in the House restaurant with other members of the Tennessee congressional delegation. The school lunch bill and a proposal for celebration of our state's sesquicentennial were discussed. Called out of the room by a reporter who wanted information on how a government release on burley tobacco applied to my district. (*M.C.* Often there are constituents as guests for lunch, and in such cases the member of Congress picks up the check.)

14. Arrived on floor of House about 12:45 P.M. and obtained permission to insert in the *Congressional Record* an article about the State Department that I thought would be interesting to my colleagues. (*M.C.*)

15. From the Democratic cloakroom, just off the floor of the House, talked to my office and had my secretary steer two constituents over to the Capitol. I could talk to them in the lobby and still remain near to the floor where debate on the school lunch measure was getting spirited. Both the men wanted jobs. One was losing his place in the Washington Navy Yard. The other had just been discharged from the Army and was seeking a position with the Department of Agriculture. (*W.R.*)

16. Returned to the House floor and made a five-minute speech in favor of the school assistance program. (*M.C.*)

17. After learning that a vote on the bill was unlikely to come until late in the afternoon, if at all, went back to office to go through the pile of mail that had arrived since the early deliveries, and get some more dictation out of the way. (*M.C.* and *W.R.* again.)

18. Read and approved a report on the soap shortage

concerning which a special House committee on small business—I am a member—had held a hearing. (*M.C.*)

19. Had visits from two constituents who were in Washington and who just wanted to say hello to their congressman. (*W.R.*)

20. Dashed back to the House floor to answer a quorum call. Many members had done just as I did: when they found out a vote on the school bill might not come until tomorrow, they went back to their offices to catch up on their work. Soon there were not enough left in the House to transact business or protect the measure if unfriendly amendments were to be offered. Fortunately, the quorum call was available to bring us back to the chamber. (*M.C.*)

21. Had a drink (soft) and a smoke in the cloakroom. (*Personal.*)

22. Appeared before the House Rules Committee at 3:30 P.M. to ask again for a rule that would ensure bringing to vote a bill from the Judiciary Committee. While there, received a call from one of the Democratic Whips to return to the floor for a vote on an amendment. (*M.C.*)

23. Signed mail (more than seventy-five letters) and digested reports from staff members who had seen other constituents, answered telephone calls, made appointments, and read newspapers from the district during the day. (*M.C.* and *W.R.*)

24. Played handball in the House gymnasium for half an hour. (*Personal*—but a member has to keep physically fit to handle both jobs.)

25. Attended dinner of the National Dairy Federation with dairymen who had come to Washington from the district. Heard speeches on OPA policy and in opposition to subsidy program. (*W.R.* I might have read digest of the speeches but I couldn't refuse the request of the constituents to attend the dinner.)

26. Home late, took the dog for a walk, visited briefly

with wife (young daughter long since in bed), and answered two long distance calls from Chattanooga that were waiting. (Anything after 11 P.M. certainly should be *Personal* but those long distance calls definitely put this in the *W.R.* class.)

27. Read a news magazine until after midnight, jotted down these notes, and so to bed. (*M.C.* Still trying to keep informed.)

A tabulation of the above items finds eight tasks in the "Washington Representative" category, eleven in the "Member of Congress" column, five that are listed under both, and three personal matters. Note also that although the actual sessions of the House and the two committees probably consumed around seven hours, the author put in a full fifteen-hour day with only the interval in the gymnasium, the soft drink, and a walk with the dog as relaxation. One doesn't go to a dinner every night, but many congressmen use their "free" nights to catch up on reading reports and gathering data needed in their appraisal of pending legislation. We think it is accurate to put down six twelve-hour days a week for the average member, plus some business that almost invariably intrudes into the Sundays.

On this particular "My Day" there were no unusual or bizarre requests such as form the basis for hundreds of feature stories from Capitol Hill every year. However, the author has had his share. One morning, an elephant-sized box stood in the corridor outside my office door. When two sweating assistants finally pried off the top and removed the contents, I was confronted by a contraption about eight feet long with a leather cover on its surface and odd arms and levers connected to an electric motor. My secretary produced a letter from a constituent who asked help in getting his amazing gift to mankind patented, and who said he was sending on a working model. The apparatus was a mechanical massage gadget.

This was on a par with the case of the elderly man who asked similar assistance in putting across his invention of a headrest that would prevent old people from falling out of chairs and beds. Another petitioner wanted the author to submit "personally" to the late President Roosevelt a new design for the national emblem. He was convinced that peace would come to the world if a dove were substituted for the traditional eagle in the government seal. When the government first started disposing of war surplus property, a woman wrote that she had heard a radio announcement stating there were some baboons for sale. Her husband was in service overseas and she was lonely. She had always wanted a baboon for a pet, and wished to know how she could order one from the government.

Some of these may fall in the crackpot category, but there are thousands of requests that are legitimate, represent useful service to citizens, and keep members in active personal contact with the executive branch of the government. Somehow, the terrific burden they impose must be lightened. The demand is sapping the ability of individual members to give the thought and study necessary to contribute to the solution of national problems confronting the Congress. Collectively, it gnaws away at the entire legislative function, and is a factor, perhaps an almost unconscious one, in the continuous temptation to delegate powers and functions to the executive departments, a trend which Senator Joseph C. O'Mahoney of Wyoming has said will make Congress "merely a timid and formal appendix to bureaucracy."

There is one important difference between a member of Congress and the private Washington representative. The latter usually has to satisfy only a small board of directors, an executive committee, or a few hundred chapters or locals.

A senator must not only make his record in Washington but at least once every six years must campaign over his state and "sell" that record to a majority of the citizens. This means he must get the approval, in many cases, of several million men and women. A congressman has to do the same thing on a smaller scale, and he has to do it every two years.

Senators and congressmen must be *both* M.C.'s and W.R.'s for their constituents. The latter function cannot be abolished or transferred. The errand-boy complex must be controlled, but what it represents will continue to expand as government grows. *Fortune* magazine puts it this way:

> "As the Federal Government reaches out to regulate more and more concerns of the people's lives, as bureaucracy grows ever bigger and more complex and centralized, this function of Congressmen becomes steadily more important. They are the men and women who humanize Big Government, who temper the edicts issuing from the vast impersonal bureaucracy in Washington to the needs and problems of individual citizens. Nobody else, no special group sent to Washington for the sole purpose, could do the job for the simple reason that the Congressman's legislative power over the bureaus is what gives his word weight with their officials. . . . What he [the article referred to Representative Everett Dirksen of Illinois] is after for himself and the rest of Congress is not *less* but *better* work."

Much of the good work accomplished by the 1946 Reorganization Act will be impaired unless Congress resolutely faces the "Washington Representative" problem of its members, and takes every possible step to enable them to discharge both their "M.C." and "W.R." functions efficiently.

CHAPTER 15

"Not Less *But* Better *Work"*

———————

No streamlining of Congress will be fully effective unless practical business methods are adopted in the "housekeeping" on Capitol Hill. The basic objective was well put by *Fortune* when it called for "not *less* but *better* work." We have emphasized the complexity of the new duties of members in their modern role of a Washington representative. It is imperative, in addition to reorganizing congressional functions and procedures, that thought also be given to the work load of the individual members.

The suggestions made here might be grouped under some fancy title such as "scientific management." We prefer simply to describe them as intended to put Congress on the same efficient business basis that its members loudly demand in the executive departments, and that is commonplace in most large, well-run, non-governmental establishments. Our proposals fall roughly into four groups: personal, information aids, technical assistants, and modern office practices.

It requires 3200 men and women to keep Congress running. Adoption of measures we recommend might add another five hundred. This addition still would leave the entire legislative branch of the government with fewer employees than were required for *any single* executive department in the peacetime year of 1939, and less than many of the independent government establishments had that same year. Our first recommendation is to apply the principles of the merit system right down the line to all congressional employees. Variations from the formal civil service will be required, but the basis for keeping or acquiring a position at the Capitol would be knowledge and experience necessary to the job, rather than the rule of patronage that now holds sway.

Capitol Hill is generally regarded as a huge caldron of politics, good and otherwise. Patronage is so traditional that if one asks some minor employee "Who do you belong to?" he will take no offense, but give the name of the member who put him on the payroll. Although here and there some individual gains the esteem of all factions to the extent of being continued on regardless of what administration is in power, ordinarily the patronage boys and girls start packing when the election returns show their sponsor has been defeated. Former Senator Huey Long carried his political influence even to the point of dictating what person should be elected to what office in the informal, semi-social organization of House secretaries and employees known as "Little Congress."

The report of the Joint Committee on the Organization of Congress recognized the patronage evil on Capitol Hill and provided that all employees other than those in the offices of members should be placed on a merit basis under a non-political system with the supervision of a director of personnel. This was a carefully considered conclusion based squarely upon impelling facts and designed to remedy one of the greatest obstacles to efficient government in Congress. This worthy provision became the chief focal point of opposition to the entire reorganization by certain senators, indicating how deeply patronage is embedded in congressional tradition. Rather than risk defeat of the remaining desirable parts of the Reorganization Act, Senator La Follette had no alternative but to surrender on this basic principle.

An impotent compromise was substituted. Thus the Appropriations Committee staffs of both chambers are to continue on a purely patronage basis.

All other committee staffs are to be appointed by a majority vote of the respective committees. The further provision that such appointments shall be permanent, non-partisan, and on the basis of fitness, is rendered practically meaningless by the failure to establish any *standards* for fitness, and by the provision that any professional staff member may be fired at any time by a majority vote of the committee, without cause.

In the equally important fields of selecting employees for the floors of the Senate and House, and in members' offices, no provisions whatsoever are made. So Congress, in the vital field of selection of its employees, remains in the old kettle of politics.

An entirely new conception of the top man in any senator's or congressman's office is necessary. The Senate wisely provided that each of its members should have an administrative assistant. To these assistants, senators should delegate the bulk of the non-legislative burden now sapping their time and energy. The persons filling the posts should be well-qualified students of government and law, and should be familiar with the functions of Congress, having a minimum of five years of related experience. It is unfortunate that the Senate did not prescribe merit standards for selecting these assistants; more unfortunate that the House members did not accord themselves assistants at all.

Administrative aides should become a very important part of the *whole* congressional picture, especially as far as dealings with the executive departments and with members' constituents are concerned. The members, of course, must assume complete responsibility for the actions and decisions of their assistants, but both the public and officials "downtown" should recognize these officials as acting for the members on the thousand-and-one questions presented by mail and in person which do not directly concern the members' legislative duties.

That is why the salary is important. Administrative assistants must be good men. If the positions do not offer attractive compensation, the list of qualified applicants will be small despite the glamour of holding a responsible post on Capitol Hill.

Senators are now allowed over $20,000 annually for office help, but cannot pay any single assistant more than $8000. A congressman gets $9500 for the same purpose and his top secretary can get no more than $5000. Yet Congress has voted funds for the White House to hire a number of executive assistants at $10,000 a year. More assistant secretaries of near-Cabinet rank have been provided for many of the executive departments. Almost every important agency has assistant or deputy directors who earn up to $9500. Congress should do as much for itself.

Members should be entitled to personal staffs selected from their respective states and districts. These employees would know the people "back home" and their problems. A special merit system should be worked out so as to enable selection of the most competent applicants from the members' constituencies.

We propose that all other employees, including those for the floor and for committee staffs, be selected on a merit basis. The Civil Service Commission should establish a separate congressional division. Classifications with fixed pay scales and merit promotions, similar to the federal service, should be worked out to cover all positions relating to work in any branch of the activities of Congress. Emphasis should be given to legislative qualifications. High standards should be set in the qualifying examinations for the many specialized jobs. All positions should be permanent, and all the protection of civil service should apply. Thus no employee could be discharged without a hearing and adequate grounds for dismissal.

Critics argue that since Congress is a political organization, with one of the major parties always in control, the personnel, especially those on committee staffs, and in Senate and House offices, could not be selected on a non-partisan basis with regard to merit only. We claim that members of Congress, even rabid partisans, actually would welcome the change.

Patronage is a detriment, a burden, of no real value to the members of the party in power. Handling patronage requires much time, always involves personalities, and inevitably leads to unpleasantness. The political support gained by dispensing positions on Capitol Hill is more than offset by the antagonism of the much larger number who apply and have to be turned down. When the Republicans were taking over control of the 80th Congress, a Democratic member happy to be relieved from the patronage muddle said, "You are welcome to this headache."

There are several successful precedents which prove the merit system can work, even on Capitol Hill. Fitness for the position is the only consideration in selecting the staffs of the Senate and House Legislative Counsel. The same is true of the experts on the Joint Committee on Internal Revenue Taxation. No member thinks of or cares about the political complexion of these employees. No party leader, however intense his political fervor, would change the present arrangement for these important services. The result has been so much more satisfactory that one wonders why it has not been applied to other Capitol positions and in an effective way to committee staffs.

A simple merit system could be put into effect by having each committee name a subcommittee consisting of two members from each party, who, with the chairman, would make appointments for the group from among those qualifying on the congressional civil service eligible list. The same principle could govern the selection of Senate and House employees: the presiding officer and two members from each party would make selections from the qualified eligibles.

In the Reorganization Act, Congress wisely ended the improper practice of borrowing employees from the executive departments. Departmental personnel, no matter how well intentioned, are bound to have the executive point of view and suffer from a too-narrow or bureaucratic approach to legislation. This makeshift type of assistance was increasing steadily before the passage of the Reorganization Act. A department usually pleaded that "we can't spare the help" when a request came in. If a loan for a few days or weeks was made, it often turned into months or even years. The employees on loan were anxious to get back to their old jobs. During congressional assignments, too often they were neither "cutting bait nor fishing."

Dispensing with personnel loaned by the executive agencies should not preclude the temporary hire of outside specialists to add to a given staff for particular investigations or studies. That is the practice today. If sufficient funds were granted, the finest talent in America would be at the dis-posal of congressional committees any time it was needed. But this temporary employment should not detract from the necessity of Congress' maintaining a basic staff of full-time, highly trained, well-paid servants.

Literally tons of information are available to Congress to keep it informed about what is happening in its own bailiwick and elsewhere in the government. The trouble is that the data are not in a form that can be used easily. Members are supposed to keep up with the executive agencies by reading their annual reports. The latter are voluminous, and those who compile them tell Congress and the people, to a considerable extent, only what they want known. But with the pressure of work already imposing a physical strain on many legislators, very few have time to read the reports. Furthermore, they do not keep Congress *currently* informed.

Congress today prepares multiple lists for pending legislation, lists which are printed daily, and which should be reduced to a single easily read compilation for each chamber. The House has five calendars; these are: *House* (bills that are up when the committees reporting same next have the floor); *Private* (private bills pending); *Union* (measures relating to appropriations); *Consent* (bills considered non-controversial); and *Motions to Discharge* (lists of petitions to get particular bills out of a committee). The Senate has two calendars: *Executive* and *Calendar of Business.*

Several of these separate calendars in both houses are clearly vestigial. Senate executive sessions, although still not open to the public, are fully reported by the press and radio, so there no longer is any point in having a separate calendar for listing pending nominations and treaties. Abolition of the Claims Committee removes most bills from the *Private* calendar of the House. In any case, the very fact of listing pending matters in so many different places is the best possible reason for consolidating all of them into two daily calendars to be called simply: "Matters Before The Senate" and "Matters Before The House."

As for the *Congressional Record,* Congress has here an opportunity to do a real, national job for itself in the field of public relations. The *Record* is of great value to members, congressional and government employees, students, and to the public. In addition to making the improvement called for in the Reorganization Act, the group charged with supervising its publication should dignify it, improve its design, and give it a fixed selling price, regardless of size, that would cover manufacturing and distribution costs. It then could be put on sale at newsstands all over the country.

Frequently, in some areas, news of what is happening in Congress is colored by the political or economic attitude of the local press. Members complain bitterly that some radio commentators give a grossly distorted picture of their work. Popularizing the *Record* would place in the hands of a substantial group of readers and listeners an unimpeachable rebuttal to any false charges made over the air or in print.

One common practice subject to abuse is the privilege a member has of extending his remarks, on any subject, in the *Appendix* of the *Record*. Some drivel has appeared there that would never have seen the light of a composing room anywhere else. Some of the news articles, editorials, and radio scripts inserted seem to be in the nature of personal favors to the writers. Members even insert poems. A great waste of time and the taxpayers' money arises from these endless "remarks" that now clutter up the daily *Record*. One "extension" consumed five hundred five pages on eleven different days. Until patriotism induced members to be more reasonable because of the paper shortage during the war, insertions of from five to ten pages were not uncommon. Such material usually is put in "for home consumption." The result is a full-length address printed originally at government expense, and a member may then, at cost, have thousands of copies of this *undelivered* speech reprinted for mailing to his constituents in franked, postage-free envelopes.

Each house should have one of its regular committees designate a subcommittee to see that there are no insertions in the *Record* which do not consist of what the member actually said on the floor; also, remarks inserted should relate directly to pending legislation.

Our last proposal to keep members currently informed is for the installation of loudspeaker systems that would make the proceedings on the floor available in the members' offices and at other convenient points. There would be separate inter-office systems for the Senate and House. It may be argued that this would keep members off the floor, but our thought is that it would stimulate attendance. It also would be invaluable to the proposed administrative assistants and to other employees on members' personal staffs. Of course, each loudspeaker must have a shut-off button!

We come now to suggestions relating to purely technical assistance. The Legislative Counsel offices in the Senate and House formerly had such small staffs that some committees had difficulty in obtaining their services until the Reorganization Act provided more funds. Individual members came after the committees, and got scant help in preparing their own legislation. Now they will get more consideration.

The very best of skill should go into the drafting of every bill that may become the law of the land. Likewise, no measure should go on the statute books without careful review and examination of established law. The Supreme Court is often faced with contradictory statutes in making its decisions. One story recounts the problem that arose in a tariff case. The law enumerated a number of commodities and gave the rate to be applied. The same statute, a few paragraphs later, listed free commodities. One particular article, the one forming the basis of the suit, was listed in both places. The Court decided that the second listing would govern since, technically, it represented a later expression of the Congress. Cases like this justify Congress in enlarging the office of Legislative Counsel to handle bill draftsmanship at all stages, for individual members and committees alike.

The other useful agency that was expanded by the Reorganization Act is the Legislative Reference Service of the Library of Congress. Up to 1946 it had a small and poorly paid staff which struggled to meet all requests from members and committees. A single request might require days of research and study. Sometimes a question really needed no answer. Shortly after the outbreak of World War II, a member asked the Reference Service to make a study of the "underground railway" used between this country and Canada during the anti-slavery fight, and see if it could "be put back in use to move secret war supplies." Now the Service has been built up to perform adequately its important job of providing legislative research on problems that confront the nation's law-makers. Under the simplified committee structure, it today has outstanding experts to serve as consultants to the parallel, or similar, Senate and House committees, as well as to assist individual members. It is gratifying to note that Dr. Ernest S. Griffith, the able head of the Service, has selected only properly qualified and well-trained merit system experts and employees.

A third technical service that could be improved vastly with a great conserving of members' time is that of liaison between the executive departments and Capitol Hill. Its value to the committees has been outlined earlier in this book. No duties take more of a member's time than visiting departments with constituents. It means putting on hat and coat, finding a taxi, or even worse, a parking space downtown near the agency to be visited, and the same problems in reverse when the conference is over. If there were liaison officials of sub-

Cabinet rank *at* the Capitol, it would simplify the problem greatly, and a member could take his people to them with the assurance that they had the authority and ability to handle most of the problems that now necessitate a trip downtown. In addition, easily located liaison offices could handle the thousands of written requests that come to the Capitol and must in turn be relayed to the departments.

Practical business methods could be used to great advantage on Capitol Hill. It is impossible to determine in advance the work load of an individual member's office, or of a committee. However, there arrive every day literally hundreds of letters that could be handled by groups of stenographers and typists in strategically placed pools. Some members have to make up a book of form replies that takes care of a considerable portion of their mail after it has been read and policy decisions made. Such pools should be located throughout the Senate and House Office Buildings, with enough in the Capitol itself to take care of committee work there. In this manner, the variation in seasonal loads, pending legislation, and the public zeal of particular legislators could be accommodated. Clerical staffs of individual members and committees could be held to a minimum, based on a carefully analyzed "normal" work load. When some member or committee had a sudden work increase, a suitably prepared request would bring additional stenographic help from the pool. The pools would aid each other as the work fluctuated, and hiring of all pool employees, under our basic personnel plan, would be from civil service lists on a non-political basis.

All mimeographing should be handled on a uniform cost basis and in a common headquarters, one each for Senate and House and perhaps a third in the Capitol building. Committee work would have priority, but there should be adequate staffs to handle jobs for individual members and all requests should go to these pools. The operation would include the services of addressing, inserting, and folding mimeographs and printed mailings.

Business management studies should be made with an eye to providing more efficient office equipment and operation. Such studies might at least produce some clocks for the old House Office Building! Other offices are equipped with accurate timepieces, but the luckless congressman in that building relies on his secretary's wristwatch. The Capitol telephone system should be modernized. The telephone staff there must daily work small miracles with its left hand, rescuing secretaries stumped as to where to call on some request. Just the same, merely to call a colleague down the hall or on the next floor, it is necessary to go manually through this overworked central switchboard. No establishment of the diversity and physical extent of the legislature of the government can call its telephone service modern, when it does not include its own dial system. That should be installed forthwith. Manual service could still be available to take care of those requiring assistance. Tie-lines with the principal government switchboards should be integrated into the dial system; they would save countless man-hours during the course of the year.

There are other minor business matters which make for major inefficiency. Under uniform rules senators and representatives should receive more airmail postage and larger travel allowances. The present restrictions on long distance telephone use are wholly out of line with modern business practice. Senators are allowed twenty-six calls a month. Members of the House cannot make an official long distance call no matter how urgent the subject matter. Committees should be allowed to use the telephone and telegraph at will, and there should be several teletype installations on Capitol

Hill. Periodic reports would prevent the abuse of these privileges.

Some of the suggestions outlined in this chapter may seem petty in comparison with the larger tasks involved in modernizing Congress. Nevertheless, in their total effect on the individual members, they probably would produce more good will in both members and constituents than any other group of proposals involved in this study. Congress, which demands better management in its vast empire of federal agencies and departments, must by the same logic put its own house in good order.

CHAPTER 16

Why Good Men Quit

ONE OF THE OUTSTANDING MEMBERS OF THE 79TH CONGRESS,
co-chairman of the committee to reorganize Congress, was
Representative Mike Monroney of Oklahoma. His job on
that committee was clearly a splendid national service to all
of the people. For this work he was awarded the Collier prize
as the House member who had performed the most constructive national service during 1945. Two aspects of the work
of his committee related to retirement provisions for congressmen, and a reasonable increase in pay. The justice
of these proposals was recognized by every individual and
group who made a study of Congress, and they were likewise
strongly endorsed by the press of the nation. Yet in his
1946 campaign for reelection to Congress, Monroney was
held up to public ridicule by his opponent—who missed
winning the election by a hair—through the simple device
of calling such fair proposals a handout to congressmen.

Such a wholly unjustified close call shows the necessity
of taking these questions out of the realm of distortion, and
explaining fully the entirely proper steps Congress took in
the Reorganization Act. We believe the facts that follow
will knock the props out from under future demagogues

who may again seek to misrepresent the essential needs of congressmen.

One of the most distressing aspects of Congress for many years has been the voluntary departure from its ranks of outstanding members. Their loss is serious on two major counts. Most of them doubtless could be reelected for many years, so the nation loses their accumulated experience and respected wisdom in the halls of Congress. Secondly, the reasons for their leaving may deter men of like abilities from seeking to serve at all.

What are these reasons? One is a feeling of frustration due to the inefficiency that results from trying to run a twentieth-century Congress without adequate tools. The distinguished former chairman of the important House Judiciary Committee, Representative Hatton W. Sumners of Texas, voluntarily ended a long career in Washington with a feeling of bitterness over what he considered was the abdication of power by the legislative branch to the Executive, and the inability of Congress to cope with the sprawling bureaucracy it had created. One of the purposes of this book has been to show how this frustration can be overcome by completely modernizing the Capitol Hill establishment.

A second impelling reason has been lack of adequate compensation, and the absence of any opportunity to accumulate a measure of security for old age. This does not mean that former and retiring members are putting the dollar sign on their public service. They have been forced to return to private life so that they could provide for the future of their families. Within the two years we have been working on this volume, we have seen Senator A. B. "Happy" Chandler of Kentucky resign to accept a $50,000 post as high commissioner of organized baseball, Democratic Whip Robert Ramspeck of Georgia leave to become vice-president of the Air Transport Association of America, and Representative

Clifton A. Woodrum of Virginia step out to direct the American Plant Food Council. These last two men were among the most valuable and influential in the House for a decade. Mr. Ramspeck said frankly that he could not make ends meet on his congressional salary. Two other members from Virginia, and at least one each from New York and Pennsylvania, retired. Candid Senator Glen Taylor of Idaho revealed that in less than two years he went $14,000 in the red.

Therefore, we endorse as basic in improving the individual quality of present and future senators and congressmen, the provision for increasing members' annual salaries from $10,000 to $12,500, as provided by the Reorganization Act, as well as the allowance of $2500 a year for expenses. Eighty-two years ago members drew $5000 a year. Today $12,500 will not go as far as half that much did in 1865. That shrewd Capitol Hill observer, Speaker Champ Clark, said a quarter-century ago that most men leave Congress poorer than when they came in.

No man can do his work efficiently, no matter what the job, when the specter of debt pays a nerve-racking visit the first of every month.

Why was it necessary to raise congressional salaries above $10,000 a year? In most parts of the country that is a lot of money. Here are a few answers. Two residences must be maintained. The cost of living in Washington is notoriously high, rivaling New York. Two sets of contributions to charities, tickets to benefits, aid to worthy causes, and many other demands must be met, in Washington and back home. Most members have to hire more help than is allowed under congressional rules, or supplement the low official pay of employees out of their own pockets. It costs money to entertain constituents. It costs money to get reelected—travel, printing, clerical help, radio time, and so on. Sizable contributions to political party war chests are inescapable. These are the facts of congressional life. They should satisfy even a penny-pincher that the average legislator is not a reckless spender or a wanton waster of his tax-derived income, but earns every cent he makes.

So far the argument has been purely on a dollars-and-cents basis. But there was an equally compelling justification for increasing salaries on Capitol Hill. In government, as well as in business, additional duties and responsibilities bring higher pay. We have shown how the job of being a senator or congressman has grown rapidly in scope in the past twenty years. An enormous burden has come with the "Washington Representative" function. The traditional duties of studying national problems, now inextricably entwined with world issues, as well as of protecting the interests of a particular state or district, have greatly increased. The responsibility for fiscal solvency of the nation is now a problem of dealing in tens of billions of taxpayer dollars. In short, the people demand more of Congress as an institution, and from its individual members, than ever before in history.

Next let us consider the justification for a sensible retirement plan, as adopted under the Reorganization Act, which nearly cost Congressman Monroney his job. There is no logic in a national system that provides old-age security for millions of gainfully employed citizens, and a well-organized retirement plan for government workers, yet makes elected officials shift for themselves when cast aside by the voters, sometimes after long and brilliant careers.

The proposal was not new. A decade ago a leading business magazine came out with a comprehensive plan to keep on paying any defeated member of Congress $10,000 a year, and hold him subject to draft for service elsewhere in the government. The general idea was that the knowledge and ability gained by service in the national legislature should not be lost to the people. Later on, a clumsily handled pension proposal was greeted with satiric "Bundles for Congress" clubs over the country.

During most of its history, Congress held sessions which were relatively short compared with the almost continuous meetings of the past few years. This enabled many members to keep up their business and professional ties and thus augment their incomes. Today, with continuing crises in the national life, Congress must, despite the provisions of the Reorganization Act for periodic recesses, remain in session most of the year. Under such conditions anyone aspiring to the Senate or House must burn his financial bridges behind him, unless he happens to be a person of independent means, which the great majority of legislators are not.

At long last, provision was made in the Reorganization Act for regular contributions by all members of Congress to a retirement fund augmented by government contributions, similar to the present retirement system for civil servants. This puts a premium on public service and will help end the spectacle of ex-members being obliged to make a living out of their influence with colleagues who were fortunate enough to be reelected.

In this latter respect the record is not a pretty one. Every so often stories crop up indicating that an ex-member is doing handsomely for himself as a lobbyist for some private interest. A former Wyoming legislator was alleged to have been instrumental in getting a retroactive provision in a tax reduction bill that saved millions in inheritance taxes for already wealthy families. A former Colorado senator was accused of lobbying on the Senate floor to secure a tax refund of many millions of dollars for a group of rich clients. Lucrative activity of this sort is supposed to have led one former committee chairman who still operates effectively to remark, "I don't know why I ever stayed so long in Congress."

But there is another side of the picture. The body of one highly respected former member would have been buried in a pauper's grave, had not friends at the Capitol heard of the family's plight and supplied funds for a decent burial.

We have pointed out the dilemma which faced a member with long service when he came to a controversial vote. Entirely dependent on his government pay for food and shelter, with no chance in his advanced years of earning a living in some other line should he be defeated, he usually voted with the lobby.

Pressure on the President by party leaders to "take care of" some deserving member who has been defeated will diminish now that an equitable retirement plan has been adopted. It is readily admitted that some appointments to the federal bench and to the diplomatic service have been made on this basis rather than on the qualifications of the persons involved. This practice should now disappear.

Some elderly members know they have outlived their usefulness; the voters realize their infirmities. But in the past, because of sentiment and the knowledge that such members have no other means to sustain themselves, the voters have hesitated to turn them out. This condition has sometimes prevented a more competent candidate from even challenging the respected but senile incumbent at the polls. The retirement plan should eliminate it.

One salutary by-product of adequate pay and retirement benefits should be the abatement of nepotism, which has always been a favorite target for critics of Congress. It never has been proven that the practice of hiring one's relatives was any more prevalent on Capitol Hill than elsewhere in or out of the government. But it is true that generally it does not contribute to efficiency.

There are exceptions, of course. One remembers the famous congressional man-and-wife teams of John Nance and Mrs. Ettie Rheiner Garner, and the late Henry T. and Mrs. Ella McBride Rainey. Some women find Washington' official, somewhat stuffy social life boring, and prefer to work in their husband's or father's office. Legislators, even as other bosses, sometimes marry their secretaries with the latter staying right on the old job.

Nepotism is a political liability, even when the relative is tucked away in an obscure position. Some newshawk uncovers the fact, and the man back home who seeks the member's job acquires good ammunition to use on the voters. *But nepotism has been the only way for some members to avoid bankruptcy.* President Truman, with his characteristic frankness, drove home this point in a news conference at the White House in June, 1945, when he strongly advocated that salaries of all members of Congress be increased to $15,000 or even $25,000 a year. He said he thought the legislators were grossly underpaid, and cited his own case while he was a senator.

The President stated frankly that, in order to meet his bills, he had to make Mrs. Truman his secretary. He much preferred that she keep house and he didn't like the idea of having her work all the time in his office, but he had no other recourse. He reminded the newsmen that Mrs. Truman's employment, which he never attempted to conceal, was a campaign issue, but that the returns indicated the people in Missouri understood his predicament. Mr. Truman concluded by expressing the view that the United States Government was rich enough to pay its employees adequately, and should do so. Mr. Truman's case is not unusual, and fewer wives and daughters will go on congressional pay rolls now that members can look forward to the earned benefits of a retirement system.

More pay and a retirement system are going to cost a little money, probably around $3,000,000 a year. Other changes here recommended will be comparatively inexpensive. This entire problem of streamlining Congress, however, has not been approached in any spirit of penny-pinching, or with any idea that the Capitol should be the abode of luxury and privilege. Improving the quality of a product seldom is achieved without increasing its cost. An exception is mass production, but the business of making good laws for this nation is not a job for an assembly line.

When other arguments fail, opponents of modernization fall back on the familiar one of cost. The taxpayers very properly raised this issue. We have an answer that will surprise many. The price of a twentieth-century Congress, in terms of increased annual appropriations to run the Senate and House, is approximately $12,500,000. This is only slightly more than the increases necessary to carry out the Reorganization Act of 1946.

A quarter-century ago, Congress cost the taxpayers about 10 million dollars. This sum represented about one-six-hundred-and-fiftieth of all federal expenses. During the next twenty-five years, government expanded faster than at any time in American history. By 1941, just before World War II, federal budgets had passed the 12 billion mark. Estimates for a normal year in the future center around 32 billion, a sum five times the $6\frac{1}{2}$ billion expended in 1930. Yet if they get good government for that projected 32 billion, the people will pay willingly.

What about Congress during this interval? The 10 million dollars grew slowly to $14\frac{1}{2}$ million dollars by 1945, *an increase in twenty-five years of less than 50 per cent.* That record might be likened to an island of economy in an ocean of extravagance. However, in the light of this study, it appears to have been a policy of dangerous niggardliness and failure to recognize that the responsibilities of the national legislature were increasing as the rest of the government made progress.

The important State Department followed pretty much the same policy as Congress, and today that department is struggling with successive reorganizations in an attempt to gear itself to handle its vastly increased problems. For years the State Department was the most economical, from a dollar-and-cents angle, of all the executive agencies. It clung to archaic procedures, and even a second-rate power would have been ashamed of some of the United States embassies and legations around the world. Almost nominal pay scales made the diplomatic service a distinct luxury. Career men could not hope to gain the top positions unless they had money, inherited it or married it. For the most important appointments, Presidents too often were forced to pick men of wealth who sometimes lacked other necessary qualifications. But, year after year, the State Department sent up modest budgets to Capitol Hill which evoked paeans of praise from economy-minded legislators. Farsighted Secretary Hull saw clearly the shadow of coming events but department administrative assistants did little to prepare that agency for its approaching war role.

What happened to the State Department when the war clouds that gathered in the late 'thirties brought the storm of 1939, drenching the world in war? It proved incapable of meeting the crisis. In rapid succession it became necessary to create the Office of War Information, the Coordinator of Inter-American Affairs, the Office of Strategic Services, the Foreign Economic Administration, and other agencies to perform critical tasks that the State Department should have been prepared to handle itself. Now, with the hindsight of war experience, most of these agencies are being merged into a greatly expanded State Department. Its future budgets probably will be many times more than the total of former estimates; even salaries and allowances have now been increased.

The most economy-minded legislators do not envision normal peacetime federal expenditures of less than 25 billion dollars. The average estimate is nearer 32 billion, and a 27-*million*-dollar Congress such as we propose will be able to do a better job of deciding how that 32 *billion* should be spent. If one considers the cost of the legislative branch as "overhead" on the control of these vast sums, then overhead will be about *one-tenth of one per cent* of the total expended.

Put the costs on a per capita basis—money out of the individual pocket. With a 140,000,000 population figure, a twentieth-century Congress on that basis will cost the American citizen a fraction over 18 cents a year: *a cent and a half a month.*

When the voters are convinced that survival of the cherished democratic form of government may possibly depend on such a small increase in the cost of operating the legislative branch, we believe they will use their ballots to drive from office any man or woman who approves the objective of modernizing Congress, but who balks at spending the few millions in permanent improvement that such an overhaul requires.

CHAPTER 17

Let's Finish the Job

WHEN CONGRESS PASSED THE LEGISLATIVE REORGANIZATION Act of 1946, the headlines shouted: "Congress Streamlined!" —"Congress Modernized!" Commentators and editors lavishly praised the achievement of the La Follette-Monroney committee. And indeed, it was a non-partisan victory that upset all predictions. It came after a bitter uphill fight in both the Senate and House to shake Congress loose from two decades of inertia that had blocked all real attempts to remedy obvious defects in the legislative machinery.

The tragic limitation of some headlines is that they omit more than they tell. The true story is seldom revealed. It would have been more accurate—but less newsworthy—if the banners had read: "Congress Takes First Steps Toward Reorganization," "First Round Won In Battle To Streamline Congress."

Senator La Follette and Representative Monroney deserve all the credit given them for piloting the bill through Congress. We join sincerely in the applause of a grateful nation. Yet the authors of the bill would be the first to admit that the job has just begun. The same is true of the brilliant political scientist who, as staff director for the Joint Committee on the Organization of Congress, directed the research and had much to do with the drafting of the bill; Dr. George B. Galloway. He states: "Taken as a whole, the Legislative Reorganization Act of 1946 took some very desirable first steps toward modernizing our national legislature. But they are only *first steps* and deal with only *part* of the problem. *Indeed, if reorganization stops here, some of the changes may do more harm than good.*"

In short, the battle for modernizing Congress is merely beginning. Congress has at least been jolted out of its doldrums, but the gains must be retained and the task completed. Public support must be enlisted for this difficult task.

The objective we urge is not merely a physical face-lifting that will send the Senate snuffboxes to museums and install mechanical devices in congressional offices. We want to give Congress real independence and actual political freedom to enable it to respond quickly and effectively to the will of the millions it represents—the American people.

There is encouraging evidence that the present national legislature is capable of self-examination and is willing to adjust its techniques to its increased responsibilities in the modern world. We have emphasized that the twentieth century has brought new duties to Congress as the legislative arm of democratic government, and to its members individually. What we fear is that Congress may stop short of adopting the remaining essential measures necessary to ensure its survival.

History shows that the destruction of democratic or republican forms of government is accompanied by a weakening, and then practical obliteration, of the legislative branch. Is it any wonder then that the first objective of a despot is to render ineffectual the people's mechanism of control in such governments? One has only to consider the recent examples in Italy, Spain, and Germany.

In this country, the average citizen feels fairly secure

about his rights of freedom and the continuation of a democratic form of government. If he had the facts he would not be lulled into such a deadly complacency by the limited measures taken to improve his Congress. He may have read no further than the headlines, and assumed that the 80th Congress started off completely equipped to meet the array of perplexing problems facing the nation. He is in for a rude awakening if Congress should fail to complete the job. As this is written a real test of Congress is in the making.

There is dangerous division of political control between the Capitol and the White House. The 1946 off-year elections gave the Republicans effective majorities in both Senate and House. The executive branch, headed by President Truman, remained Democratic. There were the usual pledges of cooperation by both sides. Even if these were sincere, there was no machinery to cope with the situation. Nothing in the Reorganization Act deals with this grave problem which goes to the heart of democracy.

Coincident with this ominous development, many business barometers and almost all economists began predicting a "recession." Dates for the anticipated "adjustment" or "shake-out" have varied. Most of the speakers and writers have noticeably avoided using the word "depression" in discussing possible effects of such an economic setback. However, to the thoughts of millions, the tragic days of 1930-32 returned with a shudder. Politically, the Executive then was Republican and the legislative control lay with the Democrats. The result was deadlock and stalemate while the nation careened toward economic chaos.

Let us hope that current predictions are not fulfilled, but if they are must there again be the spectacle of a democracy unable to function in an emergency? Can we afford again to run the risk of the people's losing faith in their government? What is the answer? One fact is obvious. Congress has done nothing so far to prepare itself to function efficiently when political control is divided—a phenomenon that has occurred no less than twenty-eight times in its legislative history.

We submit that our recommendations for a National Legislative Policy Committee would go a long way toward establishing practical legislative-executive liaison now and in the future. Other proposals have been offered here to help bridge this dangerous gap in the American system of government, the most compelling of many arguments for Congress to set about *immediately* to finish the reorganization job. One must realize that it is natural for both political factions to use every parliamentary trick in jockeying for position and making a record to take to the people in the next presidential election. This condition puts the efficiency of Congress to its supreme test. Explosive issues like housing, labor, the atomic bomb, and the United Nations, just won't retire to convenient sidelines and wait for 1948 to roll around. And one of the greatest barriers to any action rises when party lines are drawn taut in filibuster. The Reorganization Act did not touch this festering evil.

Another serious omission in the 1946 law that is haunting the 80th Congress was the failure to cast off the dead roots of a rigid seniority rule which governs all appointments on Capitol Hill. A good start was made toward streamlining committee functions, yet under the simplified committee structure the evils of seniority—with its attendant sectional favoritism and senility—become even more apparent.

There is no easy legislative road ahead for Congress. Domestic and international issues crowd upon it; steps must be taken to give senators and congressmen more time to concentrate on these complex problems, and to provide more time for exercise of the deliberative functions. Yet in addition to the filibuster which can waste days and even weeks,

Congress failed to shed such trivia as housekeeping for the voteless residents of the city of Washington. Both houses have retained their District of Columbia Committees. In view of the added importance of each committee under the 1946 changes, this anachronism becomes even more ludicrous.

One of the greatest shortcomings in the reorganizing efforts of the 79th Congress was the retention of patronage, the spoils system. A Senate jealous of its job-giving pap killed the admirable merit system plan contained in the original La Follette-Monroney bill. Pious announcements, or even experimentation with a makeshift personnel director to handle appointments to the enlarged committee staffs, leave us cold. No group of able and qualified legislative assistants can be built up unless the men asked to make these positions their life careers have statutory protection of tenure. One can hardly plan a lifetime of public service if his bread and butter goes on an auction block every time there is a shift in party control or a committee chairmanship. That is a calculated risk every elected official must take, but it should not apply to a staff of non-partisan experts on whom members of both parties must rely for expert assistance. Much of the gain of the 1946 reorganization will be nullified if this condition is not remedied immediately.

Failure to give time-pressed members of the House executive assistants; failure even to consider any changes in floor procedure such as voting with electric machines; failure to approach legislative-executive liaison realistically with such remedies as the report and question period—the failure to effectuate these and many other proposals points up the imperative need for action. Most of the changes can be effected by simple bills or resolutions passed by Congress. Only three require constitutional amendments. The question that naturally arises is: How can the job be finished?

The answer is that Congress must be shown that its constituency—the American people—is not satisfied with half-way measures. This sounds as if the authors were starting a pressure campaign of their own. So be it. However, we are not asking for form letters or chain telegrams. We want the people to think this through for themselves and then demand action based on their own convictions. We want them to watch Congress in action, and measure the glaring deficiencies that are revealed almost daily against the recommendations made here.

This calls for discussion—the very thing we want more of in Congress itself. We want discussion in homes, in study groups, in the schools, colleges, and universities, in women's clubs and neighborhood organizations, in civic organizations and over the traditional cracker-barrel at the crossroads country store. We want forums and debates over the radio, at educational institutions, in the press and magazines, in lodges and union halls. For the campaign to be successful, there must be study and analysis at every point where the educational process functions in American society. Above all, the sentiment crystallized at these forums, lectures, and debates must be communicated to individual senators and representatives. The national legislators must hear the aroused voice of an intelligent electorate, a voice insisting that there be a completely modern Congress to go hand in hand with a modern America.

The United States and Great Britain are the only great stable representative governments remaining in the world today. This fact led Dr. Charles A. Beard to write the author: "I am not . . . a mere alarmist, but I am profoundly disturbed by the decline of representative government in the world. . . . There is nothing more important for the future of popular government in America than an overhauling of

ial methods and the establishment of better rela-
..n the Executive. . . . This must be done if popular
government is to weather coming storms."

Bernard M. Baruch stated the proposition from another
important viewpoint. Said Mr. Baruch: "Today we face a
great political and philosophical issue—statism versus in-
dividualism . . . the process of the individual effort which
we call the capitalistic system may not be the ultimate, but
it is the best thus far devised . . . I believe in trying to
better that system instead of tearing it down."

The legislative tangle that exists today in Washington
does not contribute to an effective Congress. Improvement of
the national legislature, therefore, goes to the very heart of
the issue so well put by these two great public leaders. Deca-
dent democracies have crumbled before the force of totalitarianism in many nations, large and small. The keystone of
a democracy is an effective legislature.

Too many times, good proposals sponsored by outstanding
statesmen go down in defeat. They commonly do so because
they were emasculated or killed in the political traps as yet
unremoved from congressional procedure. Conversely, bad
measures continue to slide through committees, or sneak in
on rulebook catwalks, because conscientious members cannot
personally follow the intricate maneuvering, or because
there is not sufficient time for deliberation. Phases of procedure in both the Senate and House untouched by the
Reorganization Act still aid entrenched bigotry and greed.

America stands on the threshold of a new world. That
world is wavering in allegiance between two concepts of life,
totalitarianism and democracy. Representative democracy
holds that government is the servant of the people. Totalitarianism commands that people be the servants of the state.
Superficially, the latter philosophy seems to be in the ascend-
ancy because it can dramatize its powers and back them by

armed force. Democracy must meet this challenge. Complete legislative efficiency is demanded.

The crux of the problem is adaptability to change. Dictators and oligarchs can, in the lines of a famous play, call in a secretary and say "take down this law." But dictators and oligarchies can never be as wise or as just as are the people when the latter have an effective means to express their will. The democratic process necessarily is slower than the dictatorial. Its day-to-day actions must therefore take advantage of every modern device that can increase operating efficiency and speed. That is why it must constantly change its rules and procedures to preserve the freedoms it confers upon its citizens.

To survive in an epochal twentieth century that quickens its pace with each passing year, Congress must prepare to meet and solve new and old issues at a faster pace. The author believes that democratic government can be no stronger or efficient than its legislative branch, and for this reason has devoted efforts to solving the problem ever since encountering the frustrations that come to every new member of Congress. When the problem is generally realized, when it is realized that in this issue America's future, and indeed the welfare of the world, is involved, self-interest will demand that the task be completed quickly. In such belief this book has been written. We have advanced the facts. The time is short. If American citizens, to whom this appeal is addressed, do their part, America can continue to have the finest democracy in the world.

There is a line from his own foresighted thinking that adorns the memorial in Washington to that great father of American democracy, Thomas Jefferson. It seems to command the people and Congress to finish the reorganization job.

I am not an advocate for frequent changes in laws and

constitutions. But laws and institutions must go hand in hand with the progress of the human mind. As that becomes more developed, more enlightened, as new discoveries are made, new truths discovered and manners and opinions change, with the change of circumstances, institutions must advance also to keep pace with the times.] *We might as well require a man to wear still the coat which fitted him when a boy as a civilized society to remain ever under the regimen of their barbarous ancestors.*

INDEX

INDEX